CLASSIC SERMONS
ON
ANGELS

KREGEL CLASSIC SERMONS Series

Classic Sermons on the Apostle Paul

Classic Sermons on the Apostle Peter

Classic Sermons on the Attributes of God

Classic Sermons on the Birth of Christ

Classic Sermons on Christian Service

Classic Sermons on the Cross of Christ

Classic Sermons on Faith and Doubt

Classic Sermons on Family and Home

Classic Sermons on the Grace of God

Classic Sermons on Heaven and Hell

Classic Sermons on the Holy Spirit

Classic Sermons on Hope

Classic Sermons on Judas Iscariot

Classic Sermons on the Miracles of Jesus

Classic Sermons on the Names of God

Classic Sermons on Overcoming Fear

Classic Sermons on the Parables of Jesus

Classic Sermons on Praise

Classic Sermons on Prayer

Classic Sermons on the Prodigal Son

Classic Sermons on the Resurrection of Christ

Classic Sermons on Revival and Spiritual Renewal

Classic Sermons on the Second Coming and
    Other Prophetic Themes

Classic Sermons on the Sovereignty of God

Classic Sermons on Spiritual Warfare

Classic Sermons on Suffering

Classic Sermons on Worship

KREGEL CLASSIC | SERMONS SERIES

CLASSIC SERMONS ON ANGELS

Compiled by
Warren W. Wiersbe

kregel
PUBLICATIONS

Grand Rapids, MI 49501

Classic Sermons on Angels
Compiled by Warren W. Wiersbe

Published by Kregel Publications, a division of Kregel, Inc., P.O. Box 2607, Grand Rapids, MI 49501. Kregel Publications provides trusted, biblical publications for Christian growth and service. Your comments and suggestions are valued.

For more information about Kregel Publications, visit our web site at http://www.kregel.com.

Cover photo: PhotoDisc, vol. 32
Cover and book design: Alan G. Hartman

Library of Congress Cataloging-in-Publication Data
Classic sermons on angels / Warren W. Wiersbe, compiler.
      p.   cm.— (Kregel classic sermons series)
   Includes index.
      1. Angels—Sermons. 2. Sermons, English. I. Wiersbe, Warren W. II. Series.
BT966.2.C56   1998   235'.3—dc21   97-41094
                                                        CIP

ISBN   0-8254-4082-3

Printed in the United States of America
1 2 3 / 04 03 02 01 00 99 98

CONTENTS

LIST OF SCRIPTURE TEXTS

PREFACE

THE *KREGEL CLASSIC SERMONS SERIES* is an attempt to assemble and publish meaningful sermons from master preachers about significant themes.

These are *sermons,* not essays or chapters taken from books about themes. Not all of these sermons could be called great, but all of them are *meaningful.* They apply the truths of the Bible to the needs of the human heart, which is something that all effective preaching must do.

While some are better known than others, all of the preachers whose sermons I have selected had important ministries and were highly respected in their day. The fact that a sermon is included in this volume does not mean that either the compiler or the publisher agrees with or endorses everything that the man did, preached, or wrote. The sermon is here because it has a valued contribution to make.

These are sermons about *significant* themes. The pulpit is no place to play with trivia. The preacher has thirty minutes in which to help mend broken hearts, change defeated lives, and save lost souls; he can never accomplish this demanding ministry by distributing homiletical tidbits. In these difficult days we do not need clever pulpiteers who discuss the times; we need dedicated ambassadors who will preach the eternities.

The reading of these sermons can enrich your spiritual life. The studying of them can enrich your skills as an interpreter and expounder of God's truth. However God uses these sermons in your life and ministry, my prayer is that His church around the world will be encouraged and strengthened by them.

WARREN W. WIERSBE

Angelic Ministry

George H. Morrison (1866–1928) assisted the great Alexander Whyte in Edinburgh, pastored two churches, and then became pastor in 1902 of the distinguished Wellington Church on University Avenue in Glasgow, Scotland. His preaching drew great crowds; in fact, people had to line up an hour before the services to be sure to get seats in the large auditorium. Morrison was a master of imagination in preaching, yet his messages are solidly biblical.

From his many published volumes of sermons, I have chosen this message, found in *The Wind on the Heath,* published in 1931 by Hodder and Stoughton, London, and republished by Kregel Publications in 1993.

George H. Morrison

1

ANGELIC MINISTRY

Ye are come . . . to an innumerable company of angels
. . . and to Jesus (Hebrews 12:22, 24).

"DO YOU BELIEVE in fairies, Mac?" asked Allan Cunningham
of a Celtic friend of his.

"Indeed, I'm not very sure," was the reply. "But do you
believe in them yourself, Mr. Cunningham?"

"I once did," replied the burly poet, "and I wish to God
I did so still, for mountain and moor have lost much of
their charm to me since my faith in their existence has
departed." He then quoted Campbell's beautiful lines,

> When science from creation's face
> Enchantment's veil withdraws,
> What lovely visions yield their place
> To cold material laws.

And so tonight if I were to ask, "Do you believe in
angels?" I think there are some here who would give
Allan Cunningham's reply. "I once did," you would say
with a great wistfulness, "and I wish to God I did so still."

In the church in Thurso where I began my ministry,
we used to enter the pulpit through red curtains. And I
often noticed a little child in front, gazing very intently
at these curtains. She thought that behind these curtains
there was heaven. She thought that the preacher came
right out of heaven. Every time the curtains moved a little,
she looked for the flashing of the wings of angels. Poor
child! She has had many a sorrow since, and she has
ceased to look for the angels long ago. She has learned that
what she took for heaven once is only a dusty loft with
spider webs in it. And if you asked her, "Do you believe in
angels?" I dare say she might reply like Allan Cunningham,
"I once did, and I wish to God I did so still."

Now we are all going to be children again tonight. For twenty minutes we shall believe in angels. We shall believe, as Jesus Christ believed, that in the heights of heaven there are angelic hosts. And then, taking the life of Jesus, we shall ask ourselves this simple question: At what particular seasons in the life of Jesus do we discover the angels coming in?

Angels Came When Jesus Was Born

Well, in the first place, we light upon the angels in the season when our Lord was born. One of the most beautiful of all our Christmas carols is "Hark, the Herald Angels Sing." Outwardly that birth at Bethlehem was an extremely insignificant event. Nobody wanted it—nobody heeded it—nobody thrilled that a great hour had come. Yet suddenly, in the dark midnight sky, there was an innumerable company of angels, singing, "Glory to God in the highest, . . . good will toward men" (Luke 2:14). It tells us that things that seem of no account here may be of tremendous import in the sight of heaven. It tells us that all the depths of heaven may thrill with what the newspaper would never chronicle. It tells us—and this is the great lesson—that though days may be coming that shall be dark with pain, the angels love to come at the beginning. It was a hard stern life that was in store for Christ. It was a life of battle and of storm. It was a life in which love was to prove recreant and the very kiss on the lips was to spell treachery. Yet at the very beginning of it all, and before the beauty of the dawn was on the mountains, suddenly an innumerable company of angels.

Do you smile at that? Do you think it a sweet fable? There is more truth sometimes in fables than in facts. When Christ was born there were angelic companies; there is that when everything beautiful is born. Here is a heart that has never known what love is, and then in that dark manger love is born. And nobody heeds it in the clamorous streets, more than they heeded the birth of Jesus Christ. And yet around that manger of the heart, where yesterday was the stir of common feet, today an innumerable company of angels. The day is coming when love will have its cross, as the day was coming when Jesus had His cross. Shadows will fall, and money will be scanty, and little children will be very ill. But the life of love is like the life of Christ—it does not begin in shadow and in sorrow. It begins with the innumerable company of angels. Dreams that are golden—hopes that are ethereal—visions that are aglow with very heaven— voices that cry across the darkened firmament, "Glory to God . . . and on earth peace." It is to such music that all true love is born, nor do the echoes of it ever die away, even when the parched lips are on the sickbed or when the hungry wolf is at the door.

Or think what happens when a high resolve is born. Have you ever had the courage to make a great decision? It is one of the joys of every fine decision that it puts an end to whispering human voices. Take your stand, and those who have enticed you shall move backward a little and leave room—room for an innumerable company of angels. To be weak is miserable, says Milton. It is to be the sport of every passing breeze. But to make one fine resolve, for Christ and manhood, is to draw to your side a thousand heavenly influences. It is to hear what you have never heard before and to see what you have never seen before, in this mysterious universe of God. Days of dreary gloom are sure to follow, but no high passion ever begins in gloom. It is born in gladness, to the sound of music, and with a vision of wings across an open heaven. And he who is wise will never forget that hour—which, valid once, is valid for eternity—when the mists come from the marshes by the sea.

Angels Came When Jesus Was Victorious

I pass on to note, in the second place, that the angels came when Jesus was victorious. "Then the devil leaveth him, and, behold, angels came and ministered unto him" (Matt. 4:11). The Gospel shows us in the clearest fashion the wiles of the Devil in our Lord's temptation. Has it ever occurred to you as a very wonderful thing that we never read of any angels there? A legend would have had it full of angels. The heights of heaven would have been white with them, but there is nothing of all that in Scripture. Under a silent heaven Christ fought His fight—out in a desert where He was alone. A single flash of an Ithuriel's spear, and He would never have been tempted like as we are. Alone He stood—alone He fought His fight—alone with His own heart and God and Scripture.

"Then the devil leaveth him, and, behold, angels came and ministered unto him." That is the second occasion on which the angels came, and the former was thirty years ago. They came when He was born and sang their music; *now,* when He is victorious. Not in the hour of wrestling with temptation, but when the Devil is routed and the battle won they appear again and minister to Him. How they ministered Scripture does not say. Perhaps they fed Him with the bread of angels. Perhaps they sang to Him such heavenly melody as made Him quite forget His gnawing hunger. But the point is that not when He was battling but when He had stood and conquered in the battle, lo, an innumerable company of angels.

Now as it was with our Master in the desert, so is it with every one of us. The angels do not come when we are tempted; they come when we have crushed temptation under foot.

> Down to Gehenna and up to the throne,
> He travels the fastest who travels alone.

There are hours when a man is terribly alone, and one is when he is fighting with the beast. But in the very moment that he conquers and says to the Devil, "Get thee behind me, Satan" (Matt. 16:23; Mark 8:33; Luke 4:8), in that very hour for him the heaven is radiant and there is the sound of music in his ears. When a man has yielded where he should have resisted—when a man has fallen where he should have stood—you can tell by the very look upon his face that for him the daughters of music are brought low. But when a man in secret has fought his battle well, leaning upon the everlasting arm, the desert rejoices and blossoms as the rose. Common duties become nobler then. Common tasks take on a finer hue. The dullest day grows radiant as June if a man has fought the Devil on that day. And to me that is the inward meaning of what I read in Scripture of the Lord, that when the Devil leaves him, lo, an innumerable company of angels.

Angels Came When Jesus Was Crucified and Buried

And then, in the third place, I find the angels coming when the Lord was crucified and buried. They sang at Bethlehem—ministered in the desert—now they sit and watch within the tomb. According to one account there was *one* angel there, according to another there were *two*. Probably the sepulcher was full of angels, and men only saw what they had eyes to see. You go into a room that is quite full of people—so full that you have hardly room to move in it—and then you go out under the stars and say, "There was only one face in all that room for me." Love has the clearest of all mortal vision, yet love can be magnificently blind. There may be fifty little children in the class, and to the mother there is only one. And so I like to think that in the sepulcher, as in the darksome heaven above Bethlehem, there was an innumerable company of angels.

Now recall the hour when Jesus was betrayed—recall the words that He spoke to Simon Peter. Peter had plucked his sword out of its sheath and had cut off the ear of the high priest's servant with it. And Jesus said to him, "Put up thy sword"; do you think that I require *your* puny arm? I might have legions of angels if I asked for them. The point to note is that He did not ask for them. The point to note is they were not given. In simple, loyal, childlike trust in God He faced the unutterable darkness of the cross.

And then—when it was over and the end was come, and they took Him down and laid Him in the grave—suddenly an innumerable company of angels. To every human eye it looked like failure. In the eyes of heaven it did not look like failure. Heaven does not send its angels to ineptitude. It sends its angels to victorious issues. They had sung their music when He was born at Bethlehem. They had sung it when He triumphed in the wilderness. They sang it now when He lay within the grave.

And so I close with a word of cheer and comfort to all who have their crosses to bear tonight. Explain it how you will, in this strange world the way of the cross is the way to angel music. Every one of us has got a cross to carry—the rich and the poor meet together there. You happy spirit—life of every company—tell me, have you not some cross to bear? We would never suspect it, meeting you in the street. You are so brave and bright and laughter-loving. But in every breast is the beating of a heart, and in every life the bearing of a cross.

Now there are two things you can do with that cross of yours. There are two things, and there are only two. You can disown it—you can push it from you; or, you can take it up and welcome it and carry it. And the singular thing is that when you do the former, invariably all the music ceases. But when you do the latter, lo, you come to Jesus, and to an innumerable company of angels.

NOTES

The Angels' Message on Christmas Day

Theodor Christlieb (1833–1889) was a German
Lutheran theologian who began his ministry as an
assistant to his father in a parish near Stuttgart. From
1858 to 1865, he pastored a German Lutheran church
in London. In 1868, he was made professor of practical
theology at the university in Bonn, a post he held until
his death. He was a strong advocate of foreign missions,
evangelism, and Christian unity and helped to found the
German Christian Union and a training school for
evangelists.

This sermon was taken from *Great Sermons on the
Birth of Christ,* compiled by Wilbur M. Smith and
published by Baker Book House in 1963.

Theodor Christlieb

2

THE ANGELS' MESSAGE
ON CHRISTMAS DAY

And the angel said unto them, Fear not: for, behold, I
bring you good tidings of great joy, which shall be to all
people. For unto you is born this day in the city of David
a Saviour, which is Christ the Lord. And this shall be a
sign unto you; Ye shall find the babe wrapped in swaddling
clothes, lying in a manger. And suddenly there was with
the angel a multitude of the heavenly host praising God,
and saying, Glory to God in the highest, and on earth
peace, good will toward men (Luke 2:10–14).

Hark! the herald angels sing
Glory to the newborn King.

Blessed be the Lord God of Israel; for he hath visited
and redeemed his people, and hath raised up an horn
of salvation for us in the house of his servant David
... that we being delivered out of the hand of our
enemies might serve him without fear, in holiness and
righteousness before him, all the days of our life (Luke
1:68–75).

Dear Christian! did ever any assembly receive a message like this—with such a hymn to follow it—or listen
to a sermon with so glad a close? Yes, here we stand before the clear fresh wellspring of that heaven-sent Gospel that never more will cease to sound while earth
retains redemption-needing and redemption-seeking
souls who want and who can feel a Savior's love. And here
we listen to that source and keynote of all other Christian songs—that highest, purest hymn of God's new covenant of grace–whose deep significance, whose joyous
tones each Christian festival that shall this next year
follow it will reecho and renew.

17

> How beautiful upon the mountains are the feet of him
> that bringeth good tidings, . . . that publisheth salvation;
> that saith unto Zion, Thy God reigneth! (Isa. 52:7).

Why can we not, when desirous to enter into the fullness of our Christmas joy at the birth of the Son of God made Son of Man—why can we not do without a repetition of those angel words, "Behold, I bring you good tidings of great joy, which shall be to all people. For unto you is born this day in the city of David a Saviour, which is Christ the Lord"? Why do we feel ourselves compelled again and again to dwell upon these words? Why can we not get them out of our minds, however often we have heard or repeated them? Is it not because a sacred fragrance still hangs about them and proves so irresistibly attractive, while to every deeper insight it demonstrates that such utterances as these cannot be the product or invention of man?

There are some truths too great, too sacred, too divine for any impure human mouth to have been the first to utter them. As hereafter we shall find it reserved for angel lips to tell of the triumphant joy of Easter day and speak of the Lord of Life's majestic transit through death's realm, so here the first glad message of salvation, which lifted up a ruined world into a new sphere of light and life and liberty by proclaiming the advent of the Second Adam, the incarnation of the Son of God in Christ, and the Everlasting Word made flesh in the manger at Bethlehem—all this could in the first instance be committed to no other agency than that of angels. The angels must first preach the glad tidings. We sons of man can but follow them like children with stammering tongues.

This new era now breaking on the world, this kingdom of peace that is springing up with the Lord Himself in David's city, and manifests its presence, not like the worldwide monarchy of Augustus, in fresh acts of lawgiving and taxation, but in the greatest, the divinest gift of the only-begotten Son; the thankful joy to be now awakened in all people; the great salvation here enshrined for each individual in this one little child; the fulfillment of all prophetic expectations that is contained in that one name—Christ—"the Lord's Anointed"; the dissipation of all doubts and fears as to the truth of the joyous message by these outward visible proofs, so suited to the needs and the capacity of poor shepherds (the swaddling clothes and the manger cradle); and this concluding invitation to the praise of God for what He has done and for all the streams of blessing that will henceforth overspread the world in this new era of peace and goodwill—all this to utter in clear, brief, much expressing and yet more suggesting words is a task, a function, that only beings floating down from realms of light, that *angels* only can fulfill.

Oh, that their words might breathe into our often cold and sluggish hearts something of a true Christmas thankfulness and joy and teach us how to preach of the world's salvation made manifest in Bethlehem today. Let us then endeavor this morning, in childlike faith, to make our own the meaning and contents of this heavenly message. We will call it: The Angels' Christmas Sermon.

The Angels' Christmas Sermon

Here are the divisions of its several parts:

1. The Joyous Introduction
2. The Consolatory Announcement
3. The Wise Confirmation
4. The Glorious Doxology

> O Jesu! Thou bright Christmas glory,
>   With Christmas grace upon me shine;
> Enlighten me to tell the story
>   Of all Thy love and work Divine:
> So teach me in Thy light to go,
> That I with Christmas love may glow.

Bless the LORD, O my soul: and all that is within me, bless his holy name. Bless the LORD, O my soul, and forget not all his benefits: who forgiveth all thine iniquities; who healeth all thy diseases; who redeemeth thy life from destruction; who crowneth thee with lovingkindness and tender mercies (Ps. 103:1–4).

The Joyous Introduction

If as we have heard in our Christmas Gospel the shepherds of Bethlehem were "sore afraid" before that first Christmas sermon had been preached to them, what a happy introduction did the angel-preacher give it in accents that resounded in their listening ears from out his sphere of light:

> Fear not: for, behold, I bring you good tidings of great joy, which shall be to all people (Luke 2:10).

We can readily comprehend the "fear" with which that sudden splendor, breaking on their midnight darkness, must have filled these poor shepherds. It is a hindrance to their Christmas joy, which the angel would rather remove by this exordium.

And surely such instinctive fear and trembling whenever some pure visitant from the world of light has drawn near to any child of man has had a deep ground in human nature itself. Was not this the case with our first parents in Paradise? And has not such fear ever since, as then, connected with the thought and sense of sin? Oh, yes, our grievous fall—our utter ruin under the pressure of divine wrath and that fear of death that all life through makes us subject to bondage—brings with it the result that every ordinary human being must tremble in his inmost soul when the light of any pure and sinless essence first shines around him. How sweet, how pleasant, then, to such, must be those opening words:

Fear not! Fear is still the mournful inheritance of many a professed Christian. What is it that, despite all the magnificence of outward jubilation, dries up the sources in unnumbered hearts of all true inward Christmas joy? Is it not in many a case the secret fear of God's just judgment to come, for which one knows himself to be not prepared, or anxious forebodings of some future discovery that make themselves inwardly felt and heard among the tumultuous hurries of a worldly life? Is it not a trembling glance at the years gone by, with their various burdens, or the weeks of this year now drawing to a close, or the immediate future, big it may be with fears and sorrow for ourselves or others who are near and dear to us? So many, many causes of unrest and apprehension make Christmas Eve and its lights to shine too often upon anxious faces. All this our angel-preacher meets in these opening words: *Fear not.* It is as if he would say: Enough of fears and doubt, poor earth, and you poor trembling children of men! Your deepest ground for fear is taken away by Him who comes as the Prince of Peace! Fear not! a remedy that is all divine is provided for your malady, whatsoever it may be. The oldest and most hardened sinner need not now sink back in despair. All may yet be forgiven or repaired, if only you will welcome this infant to the manger. Oh, let your fear be turned to gladness, For, behold, I bring you good tidings of great joy, which shall be to all people. Who, after such an introduction as this, is not eager to hear the good news themselves?

If I say to a trustful child, "I have something very good to give you," the little eyes begin to sparkle, the little frame to quiver with joy, as it reaches out a hand for the unknown present. Such joyful expectation the angel would excite in these poor shepherds now. And never was a message that so well deserved the name of Good Tidings as that he now brings them. To a world of sinners its Redeemer is come; in the shadow of death life's light is shining! To the angel himself it is infinite happiness to be the bearer of such good news. He would rather infuse his gladness into us, drawn from the purest, fullest fount of joy. Abraham, David, and all the prophets have had foretastes of it in years gone by; how many myriads of Christian souls will taste its sweetness in years to come! And not these only; the joy shall be great "to all people."

To all people. To the sons of Israel first, high and low, and then to all nations throughout the world. And the joy is one and the same to all. You prepare at Christmas different presents—for the little ones one sort, for older children another, and yet other kinds for parents and old people. But it is not so with this highest gift, of which the angel here speaks! It is one and the same great gift for all—for young and old, for rich and poor, for the shepherds at Bethlehem, for you and me. And all that this message requires of you is simple, thankful, expectant joy! At other times other things are required, but only grateful gladness now. Will you not yield it? Or does the gift appear too great for your acceptance, too good to be really meant for you?

Some years ago a packet reached a struggling pastor in a Bohemian village. It contained a considerable sum of money toward the building of a church, and you, of this congregation, had sent it. It seemed to the good man at first too much to be meant for him or for him to accept. But when he had opened your pastor's letter, read the friendly cheering words that explained all to him and made him ashamed of his previous incredulity, he burst into tears of joy and gratitude and sent us back a warm thanksgiving. So, Christian doubter, let it be with you now. These words "all people" involve your name. Open then the letter, and see what it tells you!

The Consolatory Announcement

The message is one of infinite comfort for you likewise: "Unto you is born this day . . . a Saviour, which is Christ the Lord" (v. 11). In these words we have the main contents of that first (angelic) Christmas sermon. It is hard to say which of these words is the most significant, while each one seems more joyous than the other.

"Unto you." The message, then, is meant for every soul to whom it comes and binds us all in fellowship together. It bids us appropriate the prophet's words: "Unto us a child is born, unto us a son is given" (Isa. 9:6), born for our sakes, not for the angels (who need not our redemption), and given to us—to you and me. We all have a God-given part in this little one. First, the children have their share in the newborn child. Then their elders, who alone can comprehend and appropriate the blessing, such as Mary His mother and these faithful shepherds. The poor have their part in Him who Himself became poor and is lying in the manger. The mighty ones of earth and the rich have theirs, for is He not Christ, the Lord of all, born

in Bethlehem, the city of King David? Servants have their part in Him, for He has taken upon Him the servant form; Jews, for He comes of the tribe of Judah; Gentiles, for He long has been their desire and will now be their light. All sinners may share His grace, for He is come to save them from their sins, even the fools and slow of heart, for He will baptize them with the Holy Spirit and with fire.

Come hither, then, all of you, you children of Adam! The Second Man, the Lord from heaven, is born your Savior.

> Lo! He comes with arms extended.
> Great and small, one and all,
>   See your ills are ended!
> With His praise the heavens are ringing,
> While your star shines from far,
>   Grace and glory bringing!

"This day," after long expectation and hope deferred, the child is born! How many prophets and righteous men have desired and sought to see this day, and have not seen it (Matt. 13:17). Holy Simeon has been long years waiting for it and has seemed to wait in vain, while this day God makes these shepherds His chosen ones to be first recipients of His loving mercy to the tribes of Israel. And this day lasts on through every Christmas, so long as the angels' sermon is repeated by the lips of men. You see it in the Christmas joy of your children; it lasts for every one of you. O Christian! This day lasts on for you! Receive not the grace of God in vain! Oh, let Jesus find a cradle in your heart, a resting place in your soul this day.

"For unto you is born this day . . . a *Saviour*." That word is the brightest jewel in the crown of our Christmas message. The child is yet unnamed among men, but the prophet has already given Him that blessed sixfold name: "Immanuel, Counsellor, God, the Mighty One, Father of Eternity, Prince of Peace." All six names the angel now combines in the one name, "Savior."

Savior! Healing One! Oh, what joy to speak that word to a world of sinners—to the lost sheep of the house of

Israel, to the bondsmen of Satan among the Gentiles! But oh! how deep, too, is the note of warning! Here is your Savior, accept His salvation! Here is your Healer, despise not the remedy! And oh, what wisdom, what teaching in the word as addressed to those newly born into His kingdom! How it warns them against all false messianic expectations! Jesus is not a worldly king but a spiritual Savior. His birth brings healing for every need. Humanity is indeed newly born in Him. All diseases are healed and all wants supplied. He is indeed a Savior.

"A Saviour, which is *Christ the Lord*"—Christ, the Anointed One, in whom all the promises are yea and amen. As Prophet, He begins the work of salvation by His word; as Priest, He seals it by His death and resurrection; as King, with His royal gifts of the Spirit, He extends and perfects it. And so is He also Lord. In Him Jehovah visits His people, claims their obedience and that of all humankind, and drives out every false and alien lordship. And so He becomes a complete Savior! able to save to the uttermost! Dear Christian soul, the angel puts now the question to you: Is this Christ, this Lord, your Savior? Does each Christmas, as it comes, bring you a deeper, fuller salvation? Or are you still a stranger to His grace? Are you afraid to draw near and receive it?

Another word in this Christmas sermon answers that fear:

"For unto you is *born*"—born in lowliness, not revealed in majesty; born—your Savior! See with what infinite grace and condescension your Savior comes and claims your heart! Will you refuse Him?

> He whom worlds could not contain,
> Is now in Mary's bosom lain;
> That little Child, so soft and small,
> Has made and holds and reigns o'er all!
> Alleluia.

If the word "Saviour" expresses the greatness of the gift, the word "born" seals and confirms it. For, in that Christ is born our Savior, He is bound to us by ties indissoluble. He is not ashamed to call us "brethren." A noble branch engrafted into our withering tree, He gives new life to its failing members. The Son of God made man unites again the long divided. He is born a Savior. From His very birth He begins to save, starting from the point where our misery begins with inborn death and sin, He, the sinless Lord of life, begins already to diffuse salvation. And whosoever, believing these glad tidings, goes and partakes of this great salvation and learns to love the living source from whence it all comes, now can say with blessed Mary: "My spirit hath rejoiced in God my Saviour" (Luke 1:47)!

The Wise Confirmation

But do doubts arise in any mind as to the truth of this glorious message? Listen to the strange yet wise confirmation that the angel adds to his joyful words: "And this shall be a sign unto you; Ye shall find the babe wrapped in swaddling clothes, lying in a manger" (2:12).

What avails an announcement, unless proved to be true? The greater the news, the harder to believe it. The angel therefore, kindly and unasked, gives these shepherds a gracious confirmation and support for their faith. And yet how strange that confirmation is! He passes in one moment from the greatest to the least. He passes from the most august of all occurrences in the empire and the world—Christ, the Lord of all, born at Bethlehem— to the humblest, most insignificant detail—a manger and swaddling clothes!

But the proof thus given is as wise as it is strange. Christ, the restorer of David's throne, born in such poverty! Without this preparation, what a hindrance to their faith would the plain facts have been to these simple shepherds! The angel takes the stumbling block away and makes it a support and pledge of the truth. And that for all time as well as now. By the sign that he gives of the truth of his announcement, he indicates the lowliness of the newborn Savior as willed and preordained by God and so at the very outset encounters and refutes all false messianic hopes and dreams. And the sermon is not only admirably adapted for these its first hearers, it speaks also to us. Those swaddling bands and that hard, wooden manger, we see were prophetic of the tortures of the cross, the bands of death, and the linen winding-sheets of the tomb.

This lowliness and humility of Jesus Christ and all His active and passive obedience from His birth to His passion, what a sign it is to us, today, of the truth—the divinity of all His doctrine, as well as of the opening Christmas story.

Proud and defiant spirits would rather have a proud, aspiring ruler and find in Him a Savior like themselves; they find Him not. The humble, simple, childlike spirit seeks Him in the manger-bed of humility and finds Him there. And how graciously does our God still give us confirmations and supports for our faith though varied according to time and circumstance.

The sign for those shepherds was the Lord's poverty, even greater than their own; the sign for us is His spotless innocence, the holiness of His doctrine, the inward grace and grandeur of His life. The sign for the men of that first generation was the majesty and gentleness of the Lord's appearance, the power of His preaching, the wonderfulness of His miracles; the sign for our generation, on the other hand, is the history of His Gospel—its mighty and increasing influence in the world, its triumphant advances, though in every case, from small beginnings, like that of the stable in David's city. Oh, if anyone but honestly seeks and inquires for himself, him God will enable to find, in the very stumbling blocks of faith, supports and confirmations of the Gospel verity.

The Glorious Doxology

But mere humiliations cannot be the end of this gracious announcement. Its joyous beginning, its comforting assurances must be followed by a glorious doxology, a song of praise, with which the lips of angels close that first angelic Christmas sermon. Did they, the morning stars, sing together when the first foundations of earth were laid (Job 38:7)? Did Israel sing the praises of the Holy One at their great deliverance from the hand of Pharaoh (Ex. 15)? And shall the whole creation be silent when so infinite a gift is vouchsafed to man? How is it,

Christians, in your own home circles? An infant member of some one family receives a present, whose meaning and value it cannot yet appreciate, but its elders hasten to thank, on its behalf, the generous gift. And can it be otherwise in the family of God? These holy angels, once so ready to serve in Israel the heirs of salvation, come forward now as the elder brothers of the race of humanity with heartfelt and unenvious joy, to offer thanks for the unspeakable gift. And so the Gospel report of this sermon ends with these words concerning the choir: "And suddenly there was with the angel a multitude of the heavenly host praising God"; thereupon follows that song of all songs—"Glory to God in the highest, and on earth peace, good will toward men" (Luke 2:13–14).

Their first glance is upward to God in the heavens, their second is downward to this lower world and humankind upon it. They teach us three things: first, to look up to heavenly heights and the throne of God as the source of every Christmas blessing; then, to look around us on the whole human family about to receive such infinite blessings; and, last, to turn our gaze inwardly on ourselves and contemplate our new relation to God.

"Glory to God in the highest." Let our praise ascend to the heavenly sanctuary and never cease either there or with men. Too long have the godless children of Adam forgotten His praise and blasphemed His name. But now that the second Adam is born, who will bring back the lost, restore His own image in the children of men, they too may join the angel choirs. All lands may sing the praises of the Holy One and their notes ascend to the highest heaven with those of angels, with those of the redeemed: "Glory to God in the highest."

"And on earth peace." Now that the Prince of Peace is born, who alone makes peace between God and man, let there be peace between man and man too. For "He is our peace" (Eph. 2:14), and leaving the world, He left peace behind Him for all His disciples that they might go forth with the Gospel of peace to a world full of hatred, strife, and contention. There the disciples are to labor for the kingdom of peace, until the swords of the warriors should

be turned into plowshares and the spears into pruning hooks and the nations learn not war any more (Isa. 2:4). How sweet the prospect! How gracious the end that is here set before us!

Peace on earth. And yet is there something mournful in the sound of these gracious words, in the midst of our wars and rumors of wars. May the Lord of all lords carry their influence into the hearts of the mighty ones on earth, on whom depend the outward issues of war and peace! And oh, may He grant to you and me that inward, true, and heavenly peace, which, flowing from Him amid the storms of worldly life, shall keep us safely hidden under His wings.

"Good will toward men." That good will is ours "in the beloved," in whom God's grace has "made us accepted" (Eph. 1:6). Yes, God now sees all humankind in Him and gives them a share in this good will. How much can these holy angels express in a few words! Do you not feel how here salutation, good wishes, and kindly warning are all combined in this short doxology? "Your future life," it says to us all, "must henceforth be lived to the glory of God; your work in this world must be one of peace-making; your walk and conversation must be guided and restrained by God's good pleasure!" The best amen, the best doxology to every sermon is not that spoken by the preacher but that uttered by his audience, receiving and fulfilling what he has taught them! So be it, dear Christians, with you today. Fulfill in your lives the words you have been hearing. This amen of the angels is a worthy conclusion to their leader's discourse. "Think not," as Luther says, "that you or any of us can ever exhaust it." Life is too short and our hearts too narrow take it all in. Else would the gladness that this message brings leave no more room in Christian hearts for doubt or fear.

But would you now in any degree partake of the blessing? Come then to the manger cradle and embrace in childlike faith the child lying there. Ask Him to help you in your daily needs; ask Him to cheer you in your cares and sorrows; ask Him to give you repentance and pardon; say to Him with all your heart—

Lord, it is good to find Thee here;
Thou sett'st me free from doubt and fear,
Hast borne the wrath of God away,
And on death's darkness poured the day.
So then to Thee, my God, my King,
A lowly hymn of praise I'll sing;
Hereafter to repeat above,
There in the courts of light and love,
An endless Alleluia.

The Encamping Angel

Alexander Maclaren (1826–1910) was one of Great Britain's most famous preachers. While pastoring the Union Chapel, Manchester (1858–1903), he became known as "the prince of expository preachers." Rarely active in denominational or civic affairs, Maclaren invested his time in studying the Word in the original languages and in sharing its truths with others in sermons that are still models of effective expository preaching. He published a number of books of sermons and climaxed his ministry by publishing his monumental *Expositions of Holy Scripture.*

This message was taken from *Week-Day Evening Addresses,* published by Funk and Wagnalls in 1902.

Alexander Maclaren

3

THE ENCAMPING ANGEL

The angel of the LORD encampeth round about them that fear him, and delivereth them (Psalm 34:7).

IF WE ACCEPT the statement in the superscription of this psalm, it dates from one of the darkest hours in David's life. His fortunes were never lower then when he fled from Gath, the city of Goliath, to Adullam. He never appears in a less noble light than when he feigned madness to avert the dangers that he might well dread there. How unlike the terror and self-degradation of the man who "scrabbled on the doors" and let "the spittle run down his beard" is the heroic and saintly constancy of this noble psalm! And yet the contrast is not so violent as to make the superscription improbable. And the tone of the whole well corresponds to what we should expect from a man delivered from some great peril but still surrounded with dangers. There—in the safety of his retreat among the rocks, with the bit of level ground where he had fought Goliath just at his feet in the valley, and Gath, from which he had escaped, away down at the mouth of the glen (if Lieutenant Conder's identification of Adullam be correct)—he sings his song of trust and praise. There he hears the lions roar among the rocks where Samson had found them in his day. There he teaches his "children," the band of broken men who there began to gather around him, the fear of the Lord and calls upon them to help him in his praise. What a picture of the outlaw and his wild followers tamed into something like order, and lifted into something like worship, rises before us, as we follow the guidance of that old commentary contained in the superscription.

The words of our text gain special force and vividness by thus localizing the psalm. Not only "the clefts of the rock" but the presence of God's angel are his defense; around him is flung not only the strength of the hills but the garrison and guard of heaven.

The Angel of the Lord—Singular

It is generally supposed that the "angel of the LORD" here is to be taken collectively and that the meaning is: the "bright-harnessed" hosts of these divine messengers are as an army of protectors around them who fear God. But I see no reason for departing from the simpler, and certainly grander, meaning that results from taking the word in its proper force of a singular. True, Scripture does speak of the legions of ministering spirits, who in their chariots of fire were once seen by suddenly opened eyes "round about" a prophet in peril and are ever ministering to the heirs of salvation. But Scripture also speaks of One, who is in an eminent sense "the angel of the LORD"—in whom, as in none other, God sets His name; whose form, dimly seen, towers above even the ranks of the angels that "excel in strength" (Ps. 103:20); whose offices and attributes blend in mysterious fashion with those of God Himself. There may be some little incongruity in thinking of the single person as "encampeth round about" us. But that does not seem a sufficient reason for obliterating the reference to that remarkable Old Testament doctrine, the retention of which seems to me to add immensely to the power of the words.

Remember some of the places in which "the angel of the LORD" appears, in order to appreciate more fully the grandeur of this promised protection. At that supreme moment when Abraham "took the knife to slay his son," the voice that "called unto him out of heaven" was the voice of "the angel of the LORD" (Gen. 22:10–11). He assumes the power of reversing a divine command. He says, "Thou hast not withheld thy son, thine only son from *me*" (v. 12, emphasis added), and then pronounces a blessing, in the utterance of which one cannot distinguish His voice from the voice of Jehovah. In like manner it is the "angel of God" that speaks to Jacob and says, "I am the God of Beth-el" (31:13). The dying patriarch invokes in

the same breath "the God which fed me all my life long
. . . the Angel which redeemed me from all evil" (Gen.
48:15–16), to bless the boys that stand before him with
their wondering eyes gazing in awe on his blind face. It
was that Angel's glory that appeared to the outcast, flam-
ing in the bush that burned unconsumed. It was He who
stood before the warrior leader of Israel, sword in hand,
and proclaimed Himself to be the captain of the Lord's
host, the leader of the armies of heaven, and the true
leader of the armies of Israel. His commands to Joshua,
His lieutenant, are the commands of "the LORD." To pass
over other instances, Isaiah correctly sums up the spirit
of the whole earlier history in words that go far to lift
the conception of this Angel of the Lord out of the region
of created beings—"In all their affliction he was afflicted,
and the angel of his presence saved them" (Isa. 63:9).

It is this lofty and mysterious messenger, and not the
hosts whom He commands, that our psalmist sees standing ready to help as He once stood, sword-bearing, by the
side of Joshua. To the warrior leader, to the warrior
psalmist, He appears, as their needs required, armored
and militant. The last of the prophets saw that dim,
mysterious figure and proclaimed, "The Lord, whom ye
seek, shall suddenly come to his temple, even the messenger of the covenant, whom ye delight in" (Mal. 3:1).
And to his gaze it was wrapped in obscure majesty and
terror of purifying flame. But for us the true messenger
of the Lord is His Son whom He has sent, in whom He
has put His name. He is the Angel of His face, in that
we behold the glory of God in the face of Jesus Christ.
He is the Angel of the covenant, in that He has sealed
the new and everlasting covenant with His blood. And
in whose own parting promise, "Lo! I am with you alway"
(Matt. 28:20), is the highest fulfillment to us Christians
of that ancient confidence: "The angel of the LORD
encampeth round about them that fear him" (Ps. 34:7).

The Angel of the Lord—Guardian

Whatever view we adopt of the significance of the first
part of the text, the force and beauty of the metaphor in

the second remains the same. If this psalm were indeed the work of the fugitive in his rocky hold at Adullam, how appropriate the thought becomes that his little encampment has such a guard. It reminds one of the incident in Jacob's life when his timid and pacific nature was trembling at the prospect of meeting Esau and when, as he traveled along, encumbered with his pastoral wealth and scantily provided with means of defense, "the angels of God met him. . . . And he called the name of that place Mahanaim" (Gen. 32:1–2), that is, two camps—his own feeble company, mostly made up of women and children, and that heavenly host that hovered above them. David's faith sees the same defense encircling his weakness. Though sense saw no protection for him and his men but their own strong arms and their mountain fastness, his opened eyes beheld the mountain full of the chariots of fire and the flashing of armor and light in the darkness of his cave.

The vision of the divine presence ever takes the form that our circumstances most require. David's then need was safety and protection. Therefore he saw the Encamping Angel, even as to Joshua the leader He appeared as the Captain of the Lord's host; as to Isaiah, in the year that the throne of Judah was emptied by the death of the earthly king, was given the vision of the Lord sitting on a throne, the King Eternal and Immortal. So to us all His grace shapes its expression according to our wants. The same gift is protean in its power of transformation, being to one man wisdom, to another strength, to the solitary companionship, to the sorrowful consolation, to the glad sobering, to the thinker truth, to the worker practical force—to each his heart's desire, if the heart's delight be God. So manifold are the aspects of God's infinite sufficiency that every soul, in every possible variety of circumstance, will find there just what will suit it. That armor fits every man who puts it on. That deep fountain is like some of those fabled springs that gave forth whatsoever precious draught any thirsty lip asked. He takes the shape that our circumstances most need. Let us see that we, on our parts, use our circumstances to help us in anticipating the shapes in which God will draw near for our help.

Learn, too, from this image in which the psalmist appropriates to himself the experience of a past generation how we ought to feed our confidence and enlarge our hopes by all God's past dealings with men. David looks back to Jacob and believes that the old fact is repeated in his own day. So every old story is true for us; though outward form may alter, inward substance remains the same. Mahanaim is still the name of every place where a man who loves God pitches his tent. We may be wandering, solitary, defenseless, but we are not alone. Our feeble encampment may lie open to assault, and we be all unfit to guard it, but the other camp is there too. Our enemies must force their way through it before they get at us. We are in its center—as they put the cattle and the sick in the midst of the encampment on the prairies when they fear an assault from the Indians—because we are the weakest. Jacob's experience may be ours: "The LORD of hosts is with us; the God of Jacob is our refuge" (Ps. 46:7, 11).

Only remember that the eye of faith alone can see that guard and that therefore we must labor to keep our consciousness of its reality fresh and vivid. Many a man in David's little band saw nothing but cold gray stone where David saw the flashing armor of the heavenly warrior. To the one all the mountain blazed with fiery chariots, to the other it was a lone hillside with the wind moaning among the rocks. We shall lose the joy and the strength of that divine protection unless we honestly and constantly try to keep our sense of it bright. Eyes that have been gazing on earthly joys, or perhaps gloating on evil sights, cannot see the angel presence. A Christian man, on a road that he cannot travel with a clear conscience, will see no angel—not even the angel with the drawn sword in his hand that bars Balaam's path among the vineyards. A man coming out of some room blazing with gas cannot all at once see into the violet depths of the mighty heavens that lie above him with all their shimmering stars. So this truth of our text is a truth of faith, and the believing eye alone beholds the angel of the Lord.

The Angel of the Lord—Deliverer

Notice, too, that final word of *deliverance,* this psalm continually recurring to that idea. The word occurs four times in it, and the thought still more often. Whether the date is rightly given, as we have assumed it to be, or not, at all events that harping upon this one phrase indicates that some season of great trial was its birth-time when all the writer's thoughts were engrossed and his prayers summed up in the one thing—deliverance. He is quite sure that such deliverance must follow if the angel presence be there. But he knows, too, that the encampment of the angel of the Lord will not keep away sorrows and trial and sharp need. So his highest hope is not of immunity from these, but of rescue out of them. And his ground of hope is that his heavenly ally cannot let him be overcome. That He will let him be troubled and put in peril, he has found; that He will not let him be crushed, he believes. Shaded and modest hopes are the brightest we can venture to cherish. The protection that we have is protection in and not protection from strife and danger. It is a filter that lets the icy cold water of sorrow drop numbingly upon us but keeps back the poison that was in it. We have to fight, but He will fight with us; to sorrow, but not alone nor without hope; to pass through many a peril, but we shall get through them. Deliverance, which implies danger, need, and woe, is the best we can hope for.

It is the least we are entitled to expect if we love Him. It is the certain issue of His encamping round about us. Always with us, He will strike for us at the best moment. "God is in the midst of her; . . . God shall help her, and that right early" (Ps. 46:5). So like the hunted fugitive in Adullam we may lift up our confident voices even when the stress of strife and sorrow is upon us. Though Gath be in sight and Saul just over the hills and no better refuge than a cave in a hillside, yet in prophecy built upon our consciousness that the angel of the covenant is with us now, we may antedate the deliverance that shall be and think of it as even now accomplished. So the apostle, when within sight of the block and the headsman's ax, broke into the rapture of his last words: "The Lord shall deliver me from every evil work, and will preserve me unto his heavenly kingdom: to whom be glory for ever and ever. Amen" (2 Tim. 4:18). Was he wrong?

The Conquering Hosts of God

George W. Truett (1867–1944) was perhaps the best-known Southern Baptist preacher of his day. He pastored the First Baptist Church of Dallas, Texas, from 1897 until his death and saw it grow both in size and influence. Active in denominational ministry, Truett served as president of the Southern Baptist Convention and for five years was president of the Baptist World Alliance, but he was known primarily as a gifted preacher and evangelist. Nearly a dozen books of his sermons were published.

This sermon was taken from *We Would See Jesus, and Other Sermons,* published in 1915 by Fleming H. Revell.

George W. Truett

4

THE CONQUERING HOSTS OF GOD

And when the servant of the man of God was risen early, and gone forth, behold, an host compassed the city both with horses and chariots. And his servant said unto him, Alas, my master! how shall we do? And he answered, Fear not: for they that be with us are more than they that be with them. And Elisha prayed, and said, LORD, I pray thee, open his eyes, that he may see. And the LORD opened the eyes of the young man; and he saw: and, behold, the mountain was full of horses and chariots of fire round about Elisha (2 Kings 6:15–17).

THE TEXT CALLS our attention to one of the most interesting events in all the Old Testament Scriptures. There are several remarkably interesting events connected with the life of this man Elisha. This one we are now to consider is one of the most beautiful, one of the most instructive, and one of the most comforting for the people of God. Here in the text are two men, the poles apart in feeling and in spirit. One is swept with consternation and fear, and the other is perfectly calm and tranquil. The one is dismayed by the prospect of harm from the enemies about them. The other calmly looks above all the dust and tumult of earth and sees and trusts One able and ready and certain to take care of His people. The latter man is steadfast in faith, which faith God's children ought ever to bear toward Him. The former is held terribly in the grip of material things and earthly surroundings and thus comes short of the privileges of the lofty and conquering faith the child of God ought to have.

The text strikingly suggests a lesson that needs always to be laid to heart. That lesson is that God's presence with His people is not a mere theory but a most glorious fact. Our theory, to be sure, is that God is with His people. We delight to say that He does not leave them in the sixth trouble nor forsake them in the seventh—He never fails nor forsakes. That is our theory. The truth of this Scripture mightily brings out the lesson that the theory is a fact—a fact that can be relied upon, the most certain fact in the life of God's child, the fact that never fails. Yes, God is with His people. They may rely upon it. He never fails nor forsakes them. He does keep His word to His people.

God's Presence with His People Is Not Realized by the Enemies of God and of His People

Many striking lessons are suggested by this old-time incident. Some of these lessons I desire to consider with you today. The first is God's presence with His people is not realized by the enemies of God and of His people. This truth is forcefully brought out in the context. The king of Syria, Benhadad, utterly forgot to reckon upon God when he was making war against Israel's king and prophet and people. Men always miss it to the last degree who do not reckon upon God. God's enemies, who are likewise the enemies of His people, fail at this point, which is a vital point. They do not reckon upon God's presence with His people. That illustration finds the most striking expression in this old-time story.

The king of Syria was bent on doing destruction to the king and country of Israel. So he laid the finest tactics to destroy the king of Israel and the people of Israel, and yet he found himself every time foiled. His best laid plans came to nothing. He went down every time in defeat. His shrewdly laid plans, when he came to the execution of them, were all utterly futile. His projects to surround the king and his army were somehow always baffled. When, again and again, he pursued his well-laid plan, supposing that this time he had the king in a net, the king was not there, neither were his men.

So, by and by, the king of Syria, in great disappointment and with heart much piqued, called his men together and said: "What man do I have who is for the king of Israel? There must be some traitor in my camp. Now, who is it?" And one of them answered back: "Not at all, O king. Your diagnosis is incorrect. It is not some man in your army that is making the trouble for you. God has a man on the other side—one man—and all your secrets whispered in your bedchamber God communicates to that prophet, Elisha. The prophet communicates them to the king, and when you are just ready to take them in your net, they are not there to be taken. That is the explanation." And then the king said: "Where is he? I will make short work of him. If he be the hindrance, then the hindrance shall be removed. Let that man be found." And so the king gathers about him a great army, and he sends them forth by night to surround this prophet, this one lone prophet, as he was in Dothan. The whole army is to surround him and, with the coming of the morning, to capture him.

What a tribute the bad man unconsciously pays to the good man! Think of sending a great army after one man! Think of sending horses and chariots and a great host, with all the accouterments of war, after one lone man! Yet that is the tribute that the bad man pays to the good man. All along the bad man feels the emanations from the good man of an influence, invisible and subtle, yet strangely mighty. This, time and again, strikes terror to the bad man's heart, as well it may. It was that same feeling that provoked bloody Queen Mary to say on one occasion: "I fear the prayers of John Knox more than I fear an army of ten thousand men." There was something in John Knox, the outflowing of which smote terror to the heart of the cruel queen. So, also, this wicked king unconsciously pays a marvelous tribute to this man of God. He sends a great army, equipped with all the equipments of war, to startle and terrify and to capture the plain, simple prophet of God.

Now, the folly of this man is the folly of every other bad man. The extreme folly of this Syrian king was that he did not reckon upon God. This the enemies of God all along fail to do. This was the mistake made by Edward, the king of England. When Edward, king of England, rode out before the Scottish troops before the battle of Bannockburn, he said to the great general who rode along by his side: "Why, there is just a handful of those fellows, and we have an army that are as the sands of the sea for multitude. There is just a handful of those men. Do they mean to fight us?" Then in a moment more all those Scottish troops kneeled down in plain sight of the army of Edward, and the general who rode alongside Edward said: "See, king. Yon men who pray will win the day or they will die." They reckoned on God, while King Edward and his hosts left Him out.

Bad men, all along, are failing to reckon upon God and are thus making their everlasting mistakes. That has been the ruinous mistake of the persecutor through the generations. The man who thinks to undo God's work by swords—by implements of war, by carnal weapons—the man who thinks to do that fails sooner or later, and fails utterly. He always fails, as surely he ought to fail.

With pardonable pride my Baptist people may point to one record, and that is that never in all the stretch of the centuries did Baptists persecute for religion's sake. Here is one chaplet of glory men will never take from the brow of my beloved people. We have always contended that every man must be allowed to worship God without restraint or proscription. We have contended that the thumbscrew and the rack and the tortures of the Inquisition and every conceivable expression of persecution are all utterly inimical to God's Spirit and to God's plan. But the bad man forgets that God will not have His people to trust in carnal weapons. That would be for them to compromise His Spirit and His purpose and His revelation to man.

Here, then, is the mistake of the persecutor always. It was the mistake of Pharaoh when he oppressed Israel in Egypt. Pharaoh did not reckon upon God. Moses said: "You had better take God into your plans." Moses said: "You must sooner or later consciously come into direct dealing with Him." Moses said: "You may not always trifle with Him with impunity." Moses said: "There is a payday coming." Moses said: "O king, you had better consider Him who sits in the heavens, unto whom all men must answer. You had better reckon upon Him." But Pharaoh scouted it all and scorned it all and laughed at it all. But one dark night the death-dealing messenger, God's angel, marched up and down the borders of Egypt. When the morning came, the wailing land of Egypt, from border to border, sounded out the desolate cry of uncounted hosts because the firstborn in every house lay dead. Then the king's heart relented and he said: "There is a God, and I cannot trifle with Him."

That was the trouble with Herod, who had the innocents put to death—thinking thus to foil the purpose of God. Herod thought that by sword, by faggot, by carnal weapons, he could obliterate the kingdom of God. That way has always failed. When they have applied the torch to one child of God, persecuting him to death, burning him at the stake for religion's sake, out of the ashes have come troops of Christians who said: "We believe what that man believes whom you have just burned to death. We are ready to be burned for the same thing." And when they have drowned some man in the same spirit, out of the gurgling waters have come ten thousand men, and they have said: "Drown us. We believe the same thing." The bad man fails to reckon upon God and is doomed. The king of the olden days left God out of his plans and was doomed. Every such man is doomed.

Poor Voltaire left God out of his plans. He utterly scouted the doctrines of God and scouted them so completely as to say: "In a little while there will not be a Bible left, nor a Christian." He printed that direful prophecy on his printing press. See what has come to pass. God's people have captured that printing press for righteousness, and the same printing press today prints this blessed Word of God. And the house in which poor Voltaire lived is now, they tell us, a great Bible store from which are scattered everywhere the leaves from the Book of Life.

Poor Tom Paine, whose writings have harmed so many young men, said in 1809: "In one hundred years there will not be a Bible left." The one hundred years are barely gone, but more than twenty times the number of Bibles that the people ever heard of before have been printed and scattered over the world since that direful prophecy. He did not reckon upon God.

Poor Ingersoll, who went up and down this great country lecturing to large audiences with his striking wit and sarcasm, building up men of straw to knock them down—on the very spot where he wrote his lecture, which he was pleased to style: "The Mistakes of Moses," they have built a noble house of worship. In this house of worship, which is open every day in the week and every week in the year, scores and hundreds and thousands every year hear of God, and many believe and live.

Every man who leaves God out of his reckoning comes to desolation. The businessman who leaves Him out will come to defeat. That was the significance of that parable which Jesus spoke to us about the rich man. He wished to build great barns because the old barns were inadequate. He would fill them with his harvests and then be ready for every exigency. But in the unexpected hour, in the very heyday of his glory when he was on the pinnacle of his splendid worldly achievement, God suddenly took him in hand with the awful statement: "Thou fool, this night thy soul shall be required of thee" (Luke 12:20). Men who do not reckon upon God come to just such destruction. So it was with the king of Syria. So it always is. So it ever shall be.

God's Presence Is Often Not Realized by His Own People

Let us study a second lesson suggested by the text. It is that God's presence is often not realized by His own people. We see that here in the case of Elisha's servant. It is altogether probable that this nameless servant of Elisha was a Christian. He was daily with the prophet of God. He ministered to him. They were close companions. It is probable, therefore, that this servant of Elisha was a Christian. But note the contrast between the two men. The servant was swept with fear. Apprehension seized him. Awful dismay possessed him as he looked around one morning and saw the city surrounded with horses and chariots and a great host of soldiers, with all the implements of war. He came back to the prophet with the cry: "Alas, my master! how shall we do?"

Now see how the prophet spoke: "Fear not: for they that be with us are more than they that be with them."

"Why, there are just two of us, Master," cries the servant. "There are just two of us, and there are thousands of them. What can we do?"

And the prophet makes some such reply as this: "There is One, an invisible One, and that One counts more in the carrying forward of the cause of right than all the armored battalions of men that can ever make their tramp felt in all the world." Then the prophet prays: "O God, open his eyes that he may see—just let the young man see." And the Lord opened his eyes and behold, the mountains were filled with horses and chariots of fire around the two men.

Oh, that is a faithful picture of the situation today! How like Elisha's servant are we all at times. We look and we see the horses, the chariots, and the marvelous display of carnal weapons, and we feel: "Alas, who are we, and what can we do in the presence of such foes and forces?" And the more that we cherish such a spirit the more easily may the enemies of God triumph over us. The awful problem, the awful sin with the people of God is their behavior that is like to the behavior of Elisha's servant. Take our many fears. How fearful we can be! How easily dismayed we can become! What terrific apprehensions do we allow, at times, to possess us! What darts of trouble we see flying around us! Oh, what moaning winds come to us! And we say: "Things are just awful, just simply awful!" Things are not awful at all while God is with us. Someone put it right when he said that even God's people insist on having a trouble factory in their houses. If trouble does not come along naturally, they put the factory to work and make it come. We somehow imagine that this is a part of the Christian program, that we should be cast down with trouble.

I think I have told some of you at the prayer meeting of an experience elsewhere, where time and again I called to see an old woman who was very well-to-do. She had a magnificent bank account, large plantations, splendid material possessions. But every time I visited her, she dealt out to me the sad story of her apprehensions and fears. She was afraid somebody would get that bank stock. She was afraid somebody would manipulate her out of those great plantations and out of that splendid home left to her by her husband. She was afraid that at last the outcome would be for her that she would have to die in a poorhouse. I heard that as long as I could, and at last I ventured to say: "Well, my good woman, what if you do have to die in the poorhouse! What does that signify? If you are God's child, as you say, His convoy of angels would as surely meet you there to carry you up to the heavenly heights as they would call for you were you in the splendid palace." How she did dishonor God by all such talk.

I knew another Christian who, every time the spring came, could see hobgoblins and specters and ghosts. It was the year when there was not going to be any rain— certain not to be any rain that year. It was the year when the farmers would not make any corn. It was the year when the wheat was all going to rust. It was the year— you could see the signs now—when the boll weevil was going to get all the cotton. I have heard him talk like that for years and years. And every such word was to the dishonor of God. There is your man playing the act of Elisha's nameless servant and saying, "Master, we are done for. We have at last come to the bottom of the ditch." He is leaving God out. The man who applies that principle in Christian life and work is Elisha's servant over again. Whenever a man knows his duty, he is to do that duty. He is unhesitatingly to do that duty, and God will take care of the results.

I saw a man join the church once in another city. He was converted graciously and was a magnificent man, but he said: "I cannot join the church here. If I join a church, I must move somewhere else. I cannot join here." And why such a conclusion? he was asked. And then he narrated the story of a difficulty between him and a man in the church. Their difficulty was supposed to be serious, very serious. Who was to blame, I do not know nor care— perhaps both were to blame. He said: "The years—many of them—have gone since the difficulty, and we have never looked into each other's faces. We have never presumed to speak to each other. I wish I could be in the church, but it is unthinkable that I should, under the circumstances, offer to join this church and expect to be received." I could easily meet that argument and did so with the doctrine of individual responsibility to God. He said: "Well, what might happen if I offered to join the church?" I said: "That is not your lookout. That is God's lookout. Your business is to do your duty, to walk down the aisle like a man for God, with the inflexible pulse to obey God and leave all the results with Him." At the very next service he stood up and said: "I have made my surrender to God. Men and brethren, I wish to be with you in the church. If you feel willing, I would be glad to have a place with you." The first man to get his hand was the man who had not spoken to him in a dozen years, and in one minute the family feud was at an end. We see specters and hobgoblins and all sorts of difficulties when we do not see God. But when we just admit God upon the premises, then our difficulties vanish like the clouds before the all-glorious sun. God forgive our unbelief! How it hinders His work, and how we let our fears, like those ten spies in Joshua's time, paralyze our faith and our powers.

The True Servant of God Always Sees God

There is another lesson in the text I would briefly mention. There was one man here who was true and who saw God. The true servant of God always sees Him. Elisha was the true servant of God, and he saw God. Oh! isn't it sublime how Elisha behaved himself when the servant said: "This city is surrounded by armed men. We are at our wit's end!"

"What do I care for the armed men?" replies the prophet. "God is [my] refuge and strength, a very present help in trouble" (Ps. 46:1). There was God's man. He was like his predecessor, Elijah, on Carmel's height, when he and the hosts of Baal met in the one great decisive test as to who was the true God. I need not here recite the familiar and wonderful story.

Elisha is walking worthily in the footsteps of his predecessor. So he says in effect to the young man, "Why, young man, how much do you count God for—God's interest in His children, in His cause, and in His chosen people over whom He watches more tenderly than a mother watches over her children? Young man, how much do you count Him for?" Isn't it a thrilling spectacle—the spectacle of a man who believes God and ever strives just to do His will?

See Abraham. God said: "Go, Abraham."

"Where?"

"Never mind—go."

And Abraham went out, not knowing whither he went, perfectly peaceful, perfectly satisfied. "I have the mandate of heaven's King behind me, and it is all right. I am going through an untrodden wilderness, but it is all right. I know not where I shall land, I know not the outcome, but it is all right."

When God said: "Offer Isaac on the altar," it was all right. It was all right because the chief factor in his life was God.

See Nehemiah, he was a serious patriot, a true reformer, a genuine man. He is to rebuild the walls of Jerusalem, but he is an exile. With no resources but his faith in God, he goes to his great task. Though laughed at, sneered at, joked about, on and on he goes. He tells us why: "The God of heaven, he will prosper us." So it always goes with the man who just believes and obeys God. O friends, if only our eyes were opened what might we not see!

That remarkable Sunday school worker, who passed to heaven a little while ago, Dr. H. Clay Trumbull, tells in one of his books of this scene that occurred a few years ago. A ship was coming back from the other side of the sea, and on it were a great many people. One day the passengers sang that glorious song: "Jesus, Lover of My Soul." As they sang it, one of the singers was strangely attracted by a voice just behind him. He looked around and searched the face of the singer. When the song was finished the stranger introduced himself to the one whose voice so strikingly arrested his attention and said: "Were you in the Civil War in the sixties?"

He said: "I was. I was a Confederate soldier."

"I thought you were," replied the first. "It all comes back to me. You were one night on picket duty and hummed the song we have just sung. I was a Union soldier in command of a squad of men. That night we heard you sing this same song. Tenderly you sang the words:

> All my trust on Thee is stayed;
> All my help from Thee I bring;
> Cover my defenseless head
> With the shadow of Thy wing!
>
> *Charles Wesley*

We had our guns leveled on you, but when you came to those words I said: 'Boys, we must not shoot such a man as that!'"

And now, after those many years, they thus met. How do you explain that deliverance? God touched the hearts of those Union soldiers and held back their will and their bullets from this poor man's head. It is no wonder that the soldiers from the South and from the North there on the ship went into each other's arms and blessed God for the overruling providence of the One who never slumbers nor sleeps and who never forgets to care for His own. Oh! if men would be wise in their relations to God! If He be left out of their plans, then are they doomed.

An eminent Texas lawyer told me recently an incident confirmatory of the very lesson I am now mentioning. Twenty-five years ago when this lawyer came to make his home in the city where he yet resides, he and the richest man in the city saw a great deal of each other. The rich man disregarded God. He caroused, he reveled, he went to the bad. He lived only for this world. The Christian lawyer said: "One evening I was going up the street to the church to prayer meeting, and I met this man. He said: 'Where are you going?' calling me by name. I said: 'I am going to prayer meeting. You had better go with me.' He said: 'Prayer meeting, and you a practical lawyer! You ought to have more sense than that. You will not get any cases at that rate. Nobody will want you for their lawyer. People don't want prayer meeting men for lawyers. You had better come with me and go to the dram shop and let us have a good time together.'" Said the lawyer: "I made an earnest plea that the end of that way was death. He laughed me to scorn. But only a few years passed, only a few, until all his property was gone, the property of that God-forgetting man. All his property was gone, his household wrecked, and his prospects blasted. He died a pauper and was buried by the county." O men, my brothers, there is a vital difference between God's man and the man not His.

I have spoken long enough. You will indulge me another word. Our constant danger is that we shall look too largely at material things. We must see Him who is invisible and trust in Him and in His love. We are at times greatly cast down. We must look up. That is our hope. The text is true. They that be for us are infinitely more than they that be against us. Sometimes we see justice perverted. Sometimes we see the ends of righteousness caricatured. Sometimes courthouse trials are contemptible farces. Sometimes the saddest spectacles of the miscarriage of law openly and defiantly blaze in a city's life. You will be cast down by many things if you take short views and look merely at earthly things. God reigns and cares and loves. They that be for us are infinitely more than they that be against us. Look up, my friends, look up. And at the last, know that the day does come when every weapon against God shall be ground to the finest powder.

Job's question is the question that sounds through the ages: "Who hath hardened himself against him, and hath prospered?" (Job 9:4). Never one. The prosperity may seem to be there, but it is only the crackling of the dry thorns consumed by the fire. There is no prosperity for a living creature that lives in permanent defiance of the will and Word of almighty God. At the end of such defiance there are the ashes of remorse and the doom of death.

Men and women who hear me today, what are your real relations to God? Have you made peace with Him?

Are you right with Him? Do you see God as did Elisha? Do you reckon upon His infinite power? Are you in harmony with His will? Is your vision of eternal things keen and clear? Do you walk by faith and not by sight? Are God's purposes real and are His promises personal to you? In the secrecy and deepest sincerity of your souls, I pray you today, each one for himself, to lay these questions to heart. Take time to realize God.

The Song of the Angels

Christmas Evans (1766–1838) was known as "the Bunyan of Wales" because of his gift of painting word pictures in his sermons. Born on Christmas Day (hence his name), Evans grew up without any formal schooling or religious training. He lost his right eye during a brawl. After he was converted at the age of seventeen, he learned to read and write and to study the Bible. He even taught himself to read Hebrew and Greek. He was a man of prayer who depended on the Holy Spirit to anoint his simple Gospel messages. He was called "the one-eyed preacher from the north." Great crowds came to hear him, and many sinners turned to the Lord.

This sermon was taken from *Sermons and Memoirs of Christmas Evans,* originally published in 1856 and reprinted by Kregel Publications in 1986.

Christmas Evans

5

THE SONG OF THE ANGELS

Glory to God in the highest, and on earth peace, good will toward men (Luke 2:14).

THE MOST IMPORTANT event recorded in the annals of time is the incarnation of the Son of God. Anointed to be "the Apostle and High Priest of our profession," it was necessary that He should humble Himself to assume our degraded nature and enter into our suffering condition. Had He appeared on earth in the unmitigated glory of His Godhead, the children of men could not have borne the revelation and could not have been benefited by His personal ministry. Neither could He have been "touched with the feeling of our infirmities" nor have offered Himself a sacrifice for our sins. His manifestation in the flesh was essential to the great objects of His advent. No wonder the heavenly host descended to announce His coming and poured forth their delight in this joyful strain: "Glory to God in the highest, and on earth peace, good will toward men."

Let us consider, first, the incarnation of the Eternal Word, and, secondly, the song of the angels on the occasion of His birth.

The Incarnation of the Eternal Word

Though it is impossible for the immutable God to be made a creature, yet the divine nature was so closely and mysteriously joined to the human that the same person was "a child born" and "the Mighty God"—"a son given" and "the Everlasting Father." The divinity did not become humanity, and the humanity did not become divinity. But the two were so united as to constitute but one glorious Mediator.

Though His incarnation did not destroy, or even tarnish

53

in the least, the essential glory of the deity, yet was it a mighty and marvelous condescension for Him "who is over all, God blessed for ever" (Rom. 9:5), thus to assume our frail and suffering flesh. Solomon asked, "Will God in very deed dwell with men on the earth?" (2 Chron. 6:18)—a question that neither men nor angels could answer. But God has answered it Himself and answered it in the affirmative. "The Word" that "was God. . . . [and] was in the beginning with God," in the fullness of time, "was made flesh, and dwelt among us, (and we beheld his glory, the glory as of the only begotten of the Father,) full of grace and truth" (John 1:1–2, 14).

We can form no idea of the natural distance between God and man. But the infinite vacuum is filled up by the Messiah. He is "Emmanuel," "the true God," and "the Son of Man." "[He] thought it not robbery to be equal with God: but made himself of no reputation, and took upon him the form of a servant, and was made in the likeness of men." Passing by the nobler nature of angels, "he took on him the seed of Abraham" (Heb. 2:16). Nor did He join Himself to humanity in its original perfection and glory. He came into the mean condition of fallen creatures, sharing with us our various infirmities and sufferings. Yet He was free from all moral contamination. He was "holy, harmless, undefiled, separate from sinners" (7:26). He "knew no sin" (2 Cor. 5:21). He "did no sin, neither was guile found in his mouth" (1 Peter 2:22).

But notwithstanding the humility of His appearance in Bethlehem, such was the dignity of His person and such the magnitude and grandeur of the work for which He came into the world that angels descended from heaven to publish the glad tidings to the children of men. True, no ambassadors were sent to the Sanhedrim at Jerusalem—none to the senate of Rome—to proclaim the coming of the Prince of Peace. But never was there such an embassage on earth to announce the birth of a royal son as that which came to the shepherds of Bethlehem. When He appeared among men, the order was given in heaven that all the angels of God should worship Him. And their example was followed by wise men upon earth.

The prophet Isaiah said that His name would be called Wonderful. The angel informed Mary that He would be great and would be called the Son of the Highest and that God would give to Him the throne of His father David and He would reign over the house of Jacob forever. "Though he was rich, yet for [our] sakes he became poor, that [we] through his poverty might be rich" (2 Cor. 8:9). He humbled Himself that we might be exalted—was bruised and wounded that we might be healed—died the most shameful death that men could inflict, that we might live the most glorious life that God can confer!

The Song of the Angels on the Occasion of His Birth

Let us now consider the import of the anthem, sung by the heavenly host, when He was born in Bethlehem. "Glory to God in the highest, and on earth peace, good will toward men."

"Glory to God in the highest." The shining light between the cherubim on the mercy seat was called "the glory of the Lord," being a supernatural representation of His presence in the sanctuary. Three of the apostles saw the same glory upon the Mount of Transfiguration, and all believers have seen it by faith. The word "glory," in the anthem of the angels, refers to the divine honor and praise resulting from the humiliation of Christ. The redemption of sinners, through the blood of the Cross and by the grace of the Holy Spirit, is not only consistent with the glory of God, but highly promotive of His glory as our Creator and Lawgiver. It brightens all the gems previously visible in His crown and reveals others that were concealed. His glory, as seen in the works of creation and providence, is the glory of wisdom, power, and love. His glory, as seen in His law and its administration, is the glory of holiness, justice, and truth. These are essential to His nature and His government.

But in the incarnation and the cross of Christ, we behold a new glory—a glory nowhere else displayed—the glory of mercy. God was known before to be the friend of saints, but here He shows Himself the friend of sinners.

His character as previously revealed was the matter of admiration and praise in earth and heaven, but this new revelation occasions new wonder and rejoicing to men and angels. Angels delighted to bear the joyful news to men, and this was the burden of their message: "Behold, I bring you good tidings of great joy, which shall be to"— the righteous? the benevolent and charitable? no; but— "to all people" (Luke 2:10). And what are these tidings? "Unto you is born this day in the city of David a Saviour, which is Christ the Lord" (v. 11). Here is the Lawgiver embracing the rebels; His the glory, theirs the benefit; while angels participate in the joy of both, singing— "Glory to God in the highest, and on earth peace."

On earth peace. Not by a compromise with Satan, as he proposed when he tempted the Son of God in the wilderness. Not at the expense of the divine law, but by magnifying and making it honorable. Not a peace with enmity, for Christ has slain the enmity by His cross. Our peace flows from the reconciling blood of Jesus. Nothing else could satisfy the claims of divine justice and procure pardon for the penitent believer.

Without the Atonement, there is no peace for sinners. There is an accusing witness within. Behold that king in the banqueting house! Why does his countenance change? Why do his knees tremble? Have the wise men of Babylon interpreted the mystic writing upon the wall? No; but conscience has. Conscience has given dreadful intimations of its meaning before Daniel comes into the presence of the king, and the Hebrew prophet only confirms the previous interpretation. Every sinner bears about with him that internal tormentor. It may be bribed, but not forever. It may be lulled to sleep, but it will awake with increased energy and augmented wrath. The gnawing worm may be stupefied for a season but cannot be killed. The devouring fire may be temporarily stifled but cannot be quenched. How dreadful are its torments when it wreaks all its anger upon the guilty! To be drowned in the Red Sea, like Pharaoh; to be swallowed up by the earth, like Korah; to be hewn in pieces, like Agag; to be eaten of worms, like Herod, is nothing in the comparison.

Where shall we find peace? We have heard of a stone that nothing but blood can dissolve. Such a stone is the human conscience. But all the blood shed on Jewish altars could never effect the work. It must be the blood of Jesus. He is "the Lamb of God that taketh away the sin of the world." At His cross the believer's conscience finds assurance and repose. He is the Good Physician, and His blood is the sovereign balm. Come to His extended arms! Come, for He waits to be gracious!

"Good will toward men." The "good will" of whom? Of God, blessed forever. The funds of a benevolent society may be exhausted, so that its members in distress can receive no benefit. But in the good will of God we find unsearchable riches of grace, sufficient to pay off our whole debt to the Law and restore our forfeited inheritance; to bring forth the prisoners and them that sit in darkness, out of the prison house; to support the believer through life, comfort him in death, and raise him from the grave not a beggar or a pensioner but a prince clothed in white and entitled to an everlasting kingdom.

Did I possess the nature of angels with my present sinfulness, I would have no hope of salvation, for God has provided no mercy for fallen angels. But, in His infinite wisdom, He has devised a method for the consistent display of His good will toward men by assuming their nature and in that nature atoning for their sins. This is a wonderful scheme, whereby God can be just and yet justify the ungodly. His law is honored, though its violator be acquitted; His government is secure, though the rebel be forgiven.

I think I hear the infant in Bethlehem speaking from the manger in the strain of the Evangelical Prophet: "Is my hand shortened at all, that it cannot redeem? or have I no power to deliver? behold, at my rebuke I dry up the sea, I make the rivers a wilderness. . . . I clothe the heavens with blackness, and I make sackcloth their covering" (Isa. 50:2–3). Though you see Me in human flesh, I am still Lord of all, and can "save them to the uttermost" (Heb. 7:25). Though you do not hear Me, I have "the tongue of the learned . . . to speak a word in season to him that is weary" (Isa. 50:4). I have taken upon Myself your nature that I may be able to sympathize in your sufferings and make satisfaction for your sins. For you will I give my back to the smiters, and my cheeks to them that pluck off the hair. I will not hide my face from shame and spitting (see v. 6). Calvary and Joseph's grave shall manifest My benevolence, and it shall be seen that My mercy is mightier than death. "Who will contend with me? . . . let him come near" (v. 8)! Let us stand together! I challenge all the powers of darkness to defeat the purposes of My grace. I will triumph by suffering. I will "dash them in pieces like a potter's vessel" (Ps. 2:9). Hell shall tremble at the report. On every gate and door post, in all My journey from this place to Golgotha and thence home to My Father's house, shall be inscribed the record of My good will toward men!

"This is a faithful saying, and worthy of all acceptation, that Christ Jesus came into the world to save sinners" (1 Tim. 1:15). Behold Him pressing the wine of eternal life for us from the cup of His own mortality. Behold Him demolishing the kingdom of darkness on earth and establishing in its stead the kingdom of heaven. Behold Him destroying the works of the Devil, delivering the captives from his iron yoke, and uniting sinners to Himself in everlasting fellowship and love. The whole economy of divine grace, based on the incarnation of the Son of God, is like a complicated piece of machinery, consisting of many wheels, all revolving in harmony and impelled by the same power. Salvation is a river flowing from the manger in Bethlehem, conveying eternal life to millions, and bearing away many a precious gem from the dominions of death and hell. It has already swept from the earth more false gods than would have filled the Roman pantheon and carried multitudes of human souls, pardoned and purified, to Abraham's bosom. No opposition of men or of devils can stand before "the glorious gospel of the blessed God" (v. 11). O that its light may shine into the heart and the conscience of every hearer! May the goodness of God lead you all to repentance and fill you with peace in believing! Then will you go forth with joy and publish His good will toward men. When the purposes of His mercy are accomplished in your hearts, you shall be removed from grace to glory— from peace to perfect love—and sin and sorrow shall be shut out forever! Amen.

The Return of the Angels

George H. Morrison (1866–1928) assisted the great Alexander Whyte in Edinburgh, pastored two churches, and then became pastor in 1902 of the distinguished Wellington Church on University Avenue in Glasgow, Scotland. His preaching drew great crowds; in fact, people had to line up an hour before the services to be sure to get seats in the large auditorium. Morrison was a master of imagination in preaching, yet his messages are solidly biblical.

From his many published volumes of sermons, I have chosen this message, found in *The Return of the Angels,* published in 1909 by Hodder and Stoughton, London.

George H. Morrison

6

THE RETURN OF THE ANGELS

And he dreamed, and behold a ladder set up on the earth, and the top of it reached to heaven: and behold the angels of God ascending and descending on it (Genesis 28:12).

And Jacob went on his way, and the angels of God met him (Genesis 32:1).

WELL-NIGH TWENTY years had passed away since Jacob had had his vision at Bethel. They had been years of hard and constant labor; they had been years of remarkable prosperity. No longer was Jacob an empty-handed fugitive, leaving his home for an uncertain future. God had been with him and had advanced him wonderfully, and He had blessed him in his basket and his store. And now he was a rich and prosperous man, master of herds and flocks innumerable and with a host of servants at his call ready to further him in every venture. There are men who prosper and who pay for prospering by never seeing the angels anymore. They win their fortune, but they lose their vision, and so are they poorer than at twenty-one. But Jacob, for all his cunning shrewdness, was not the man to lose his hold on God. He had a heart that thirsted after God even in his most worldly and successful days. Now he was on his way home to Canaan, and as he journeyed, the angels of God met him. This was the second time, for—twenty years before—had they not flashed upon his sight at Bethel? And what I want to do tonight is this: First, I want to look at these two angelic visits; secondly, to show you how they differed from one another; and thirdly, to see how these differences have their meanings still.

First Vision Among the Hills—
Second Vision upon the Trodden Highway

First, then, the former angels were seen among the hills but the latter upon the trodden highway.

We can readily picture the scenery at Bethel where Jacob saw the ladder to the heavens. It was a place of wild and rugged grandeur, touched with the mystery of highland solitudes. At home, in the pastureland of rich Beersheba, his eye had looked out upon the rolling downs.. There was nothing sublime or awful at Beersheba. It was a sweet and satisfying prospect. But here it was different. Here there were rugged cliffs and rock piled upon rock in wild confusion. It was here among the hills of Bethel that Jacob had his first vision of the angels. It was a resting place of highland grandeur, and the spirit of Jacob was uplifted by it. He was thrilled with the high sense of the sublime as he lay down amid the loneliness of nature. But it was not amid a grandeur such as that, that he had his vision when twenty years were gone—he went on his way and the angels of God met him. He was no longer a romantic youth; he was a conventional and unromantic wayfarer. The road was familiar, hard, and dusty, and there was none of the mystery of Bethel here. And yet the angels who had shone at Bethel, in the delicious hour of freedom and of youth, came back again on to the common road where feet were plodding along wearily.

Now it seems to me that, if we are living wisely, we ought all to have an experience like Jacob. If we have had our hour at Bethel once, we ought also to have our Mahanaim. Most of us have had our moments on the mount when we knew that heaven was not far away. Then we felt intensely and saw clearly, and life was exquisitely rich and full. Such was the joy and wonder of it all, when we were bathed in the deep flood of being, that we were ready to cry as Jacob cried, "This is none other but the house of God, and this is the gate of heaven" (Gen. 28:17). It is a great thing to see the angels then, and life shall never be the same if we have seen them. Yet how rarely do such moments come, matched with our days of uneventful journey! And this is the glad thing about human life, that if we are brave and steadfast in unillumined days, like Jacob we shall go upon our journeys and the angels of God shall meet with us again. God may be near us when we are inspired, but God is just as near when we are faithful. The man who climbs may have his glimpse of heaven, but so has the man who simply pushes on.

And that is the test and triumph of religion—not that it irradiates golden moments but that it comes with music and with ministry into the dusty highroad of today. We all grow weary of the routine sometimes. We are tempted to break away and take our liberty. But it was not when Jacob broke into his liberty that the angels of God met with him again. It was when Jacob went upon his way and quietly and doggedly pushed on, taking the homeward road and doing his duty although seductive voices were calling. Am I speaking to anyone tonight who is restless or who is on the point of throwing it all over? Do not do that, my friend. That is cowardice. That is to turn your back on all the angels. Take up your cross. Go to your task again. Bethel is in the past and gone forever. But still, like Jacob, you may have Mahanaim and the angels who meet us in the way.

First Vision in Solitude—
Second Vision in Society

The former vision came in solitude but the latter vision in society. That is another difference to be noted between Bethel and Mahanaim. At Bethel Jacob was utterly alone. For the first time in his life he was alone. He was an exile now from the old tent where he had passed the happy days of boyhood. And at that very hour (for it was sundown) his brother Esau would be wending homeward, and his aged father would be awaiting him, while his mother would be busy in the tent. It is such memories that make us lonely. It was such memories that made Jacob lonely. He saw his home again and heard its voices. It was night and around him were the hills. And it was then in such an hour of solitude, when he might cry and there was none to answer, that Jacob had his vision of the angels. Do you see the difference at Mahanaim? Jacob was not solitary now. His wife was there; his family was there; his servants and his shepherds were about him. The road was noisy with the stir of life—shouting of drover and lowing of the herd—and now there was a snatch of song and the laughter of his merry children. At Bethel there was utter solitude, at Mahanaim was society. At Bethel there was none to answer, at Mahanaim there were happy voices. The point to note is that the angels, who flashed upon the solitude at Bethel, came back again amid that circle.

And that is what the angels always do, if we but keep ourselves in tune with heaven. They flash upon us first when we are solitary, and then we catch their radiance in society. A man is always utterly alone when personal religion takes its rise. He is alone with God, alone with his own heart, alone with his own sin and with his past. And no one knows what misery he feels, nor how the Spirit is striving with his soul, nor how he is crying out to God for mercy. One by one we are born into the world, and one by one we are born into the kingdom. Strait is the gate that opens upon life, so strait that two cannot enter it abreast.

Yet the glad thing about our faith is this, that having made our peace with God in Christ, we go on the way amid familiar faces and the angels meet with us again. There is something new in the familiar home. There is a new nobility in love. Wherever children are, there is mystery; wherever there is sorrow, there is sanctity. Common life cannot be common now since Jesus Christ has stooped to enter it. And on the least and lowest there is glory, since for the least and lowest Jesus died. That is the meaning of our Mahanaim. It is the angel amid familiar faces. It is the vision of what is bright and fair, as we take our way among our friends and family. And Mahanaim always follows Bethel—the hour when we have been alone with God, heard Him speak to us, trusted Him, and seen the shining ladder to the throne.

First Vision on a Shining Staircase—
Second Vision Armed for War

In closing, there is another difference, perhaps the most significant of all. At Bethel the angels were on a shining staircase, at Mahanaim they were armed for war. Do you detect the meaning of that difference? Do you see the parable of God in it? Do you understand why first they climbed the steps and then were marshaled as a fighting legion? Let me try to explain to you that difficulty.

Well, think of Jacob when he came to Bethel. Try to picture what was in his heart. He was separated from his father's dwelling now, and he felt separated from his father's God. Jewish religion was family religion. It clung with a great passion to the home. When a man turned his back upon the home, it was like turning his back upon the promise. And every fresh league that Jacob traveled not only left him further from his mother but left him with the desolating sense that he was further from his mother's God. Such was the past. What about the future? The future was shrouded in uncertainty. Jacob was not afraid—no young man is afraid when he goes out to battle with the world. But *there* were the hills and up them he must climb, yet what might be beyond them was unknown. So, uncertain, Jacob fell asleep. It was then that there shone on him the ladder, and the foot of the ladder was his rocky bed. It did not rise from the far-distant tent. It rose from the very spot where he was sleeping. There where he lay, alone among the hills, he was as near to God as at Beersheba. Let him travel anywhere and everywhere, he might be certain God was with him now. Was it not that which Jacob needed? You see the angels gave him what he needed. They gave him fellowship when he was lonely. They gave him heaven when he was far from home. They gave him hope that he might rise and journey, not knowing where he might find himself at nightfall, yet sure that God was ordering his way and would never leave him nor forsake him.

Now turn from Bethel to that other scene when the angels met with him again. Do you know what was in

Jacob's heart that day? Jacob was possessed by a great fear. Yonder was Edom where his brother dwelt—his brother Esau whom he had wronged so terribly. Had he not stolen his birthright long ago, and was it likely that Esau had forgiven him? And in a little he must meet with Esau. Now Esau was a man of war, but Jacob had grown soft in his prosperity and was better at a bargain than a battle. He was afraid. His conscience was at work, and conscience does make cowards of us all. If Esau fell on him in wild revenge, what hope was there for Jacob and his company? And it was then that Jacob saw the angels and saw them as an armed host above him. He heard the rushing of a thousand chariots and caught the flashing of a thousand spears. They were not mounting on the golden staircase; they were marshaled in the ranks of war. They were not moving up and down the ladder; they were mustered to do battle for him. And what I say is that it was just that vision which Jacob needed in his hour of trembling. It made him far more powerful than Esau, for around him were the legions of his God.

And so we learn the old and precious lesson that God reveals Himself just as we need Him. He never gives us what we shall want tomorrow; He gives us richly what we need today. Just as water, poured into twenty goblets, will take the different shape of every goblet, so the grace of God poured into twenty days will fill the different need of every day. And that is why Christ, who knows the Father's heart, bids us never be anxious for tomorrow—"Give us *this day* our daily bread" (Matt. 6:11, emphasis added). When we need the ladder, we shall have the ladder. When we require the army, we shall get it. We shall have grace to live by, while we are called to live. We shall have grace to die by, when we are called to die. It was that faith which buoyed the heart of Jacob, carried him forward, and made him more than conqueror. It is that faith which you and I must have if life is to be victorious and serene.

NOTES

The Sympathy of the Two Worlds

Charles Haddon Spurgeon (1834–1892) is undoubtedly the most famous minister of the nineteenth century. Converted in 1850, he united with the Baptists and soon began to preach in various places. He became pastor of the Baptist church in Waterbeach, England, in 1851, and three years later he was called to the decaying Park Street Church, London. Within a short time the work began to prosper, a new church was built and dedicated in 1861, and Spurgeon became London's most popular preacher. In 1855, he began to publish his sermons weekly; today they make up the fifty-seven volumes of *The Metropolitan Tabernacle Pulpit*. He founded a pastor's college and several orphanages.

This sermon was taken from *The New Park Street Pulpit,* volume 4.

Charles Haddon Spurgeon

7

THE SYMPATHY OF
THE TWO WORLDS

There is joy in the presence of the angels of God over
one sinner that repenteth (Luke 15:10).

MAN'S HEART IS never big enough to hold either its joys or
its sorrows. You never heard of a man whose heart was
exactly full of sorrow, for no sooner is it full than it
overflows. The first prompting of the soul is to tell its
sorrow to another. The reason is that the heart is not
large enough to hold our grief, and we need to have
another heart to receive a portion thereof. It is even so
with our joy. When the heart is full of joy, it always allows
its joy to escape. It is like the fountain in the marketplace.
Whenever the fountain is full it runs away in streams,
and as soon as it ceases to overflow, you may be quite
sure that it has ceased to be full. The only full heart is
the overflowing heart.

You know this, beloved. You have proved it to be true.
For when your soul has been full of joy, you have first
called together your own kindred and friends and have
communicated to them the cause of your gladness. When
those vessels have been full even to the brim, you have
been like the woman who borrowed empty vessels of her
neighbors, for you have asked each of them to become
partakers in your joy. And when the hearts of all your
neighbors have been full, you have felt as if they were
not large enough, and the whole world has been called
upon to join in your praise. You bade the fathomless
ocean drink in your joy. You spoke to the trees and bade
them clap their hands, while the mountains and hills
were invoked by you to break forth into singing. The very
stars of heaven seemed to look down upon you, and you
bade them sing for you. All the world was full of music

through the music that was in your heart. And, after all, what is man but the great musician of the world?

The universe is a great organ with mighty pipes. Space, time, eternity are like the throats of this great organ. And man, a little creature, puts his fingers on the keys and wakes the universe to thunders of harmony, stirring up the whole creation to mightiest acclamations of praise. Do you not know that man is God's high priest in the universe? All things else are but the sacrifice, but he is the priest—carrying in his heart the fire and in his hand the wood and in his mouth the two-edged sword of dedication, with which he offers up all things to God.

But I have no doubt, beloved, the thought has sometimes struck us that our praise does not go far enough. We seem as if we have dwelt in an island cut off from the mainland. This world, like a fair planet, swims in a sea of ether unnavigated by mortal ship. We have sometimes thought that surely our praise was confined to the shores of this poor narrow world, that it was impossible for us to pull the ropes that might ring the bells of heaven, that we could by no means whatever reach our hands so high as to sweep the celestial chords of angelic harps. We have said to ourselves there is no connection between earth and heaven. A huge black wall divides us. A strait of unnavigable waters shuts us out. Our prayers cannot reach to heaven, neither can our praises affect the celestials. Let us learn from our text how mistaken we are. We are, after all, however much we seem to be shut out from heaven and from the great universe but a province of God's vast united empire. What is done on earth is known in heaven; what is sung on earth is sung in heaven. There is a sense in which it is true that the tears of earth are wept again in paradise, and the sorrows of humankind are felt again, even on the throne of the Most High.

My text tells us, "There is joy in the presence of the angels of God over one sinner that repenteth." It seems as if it showed me a bridge by which I might cross over into eternity. It does, as it were, exhibit to me certain magnetic wires that convey the intelligence of what is done here to spirits in another world. It teaches me that there is a real and wonderful connection between this lower world and that which is beyond the skies, where God dwells in the land of the happy.

We shall talk about that subject a little this morning. My first head will be *the sympathy of the world above with the world below*. The second head will be *the judgment of the angels*—they rejoice over repenting sinners. We shall see what is their ground for doing so. The third head will be *a lesson for the saints*. If the angels in heaven rejoice over repenting sinners, so should we.

The Sympathy of the World Above with the World Below

In the first place, our text teaches us the sympathy of the two worlds. Imagine not, O beloved, that you are cut off from heaven, for there is a ladder—the top of which rests at the foot of the throne of the Almighty, and the base of which is fixed in the lowest place of man's misery! Conceive not that there is a great gulf fixed between you and the Father, across which His mercy cannot come and over which your prayers and faith can never leap. Oh, think not, beloved, that you dwell in a storm-girt island cut off from the continent of eternity. I beseech you, believe that there is a bridge across that chasm, a road along which feet may travel. This world is not separated, for all creation is but one body. And know that though you do but dwell in this road, as it were on the foot, yet from the feet even to the head there are nerves and veins that do unite the whole. The same great heart that beats in heaven beats on earth. The love of the eternal Father that cheers the celestial makes glad the terrestrial, too. Rest assured that though the glory of the celestial be one and the glory of the terrestrial be another, yet are they but another in appearance, for after all, they are the same. O listen, and you will soon learn that you are no stranger in a strange land—a houseless Joseph in the land of Egypt, shut out from his father and his children, who still remain in the happy paradise of Canaan. No, your Father loves you still. There is a connection between you and Him.

Strange that though leagues of distance lie between the finite creature and the infinite Creator, yet there are links that unite us both! When a tear is wept by you, think not that your Father does not behold it, for, "Like as a Father pitieth his children so the LORD pitieth them that fear him" (Ps. 103:13). Your sigh is able to move the heart of Jehovah; your whisper can incline His ear to you; your prayer can stay His hands; your faith can move His arm. Oh! think not that God sits on high in an eternal slumber taking no account of you. "Can a woman forget her sucking child, that she should not have compassion on the son of her womb? yea, they may forget, yet will I not forget thee" (Isa. 49:15). Engraven upon the Father's hand your name remains, and on His heart recorded there your person stands. He thought of you before the worlds were made. Before the channels of the sea were scooped or the gigantic mountains lifted their heads in the white clouds, He thought of you. He thinks about you still. "I the LORD do keep it; I will water it every moment: lest any hurt it, I will keep it night and day" (27:3). For the eyes of the Lord run to and fro in every place to show Himself strong on the behalf of all them that fear Him. You are not cut off from Him. You move in Him. In Him you live and have your being. "God is . . . a very present help in trouble" (Ps. 46:1).

Remember, again, O heir of immortality, that you are not only linked to the Godhead, but there is another one in heaven with whom you have a strange yet near connection. In the center of the throne sits one who is your brother, allied to you by blood. The Son of God—eternal, equal with His Father—became in the fullness of time the son of Mary, an infant of a span long. He was, yea is, bone of your bone and flesh of your flesh. Think not that you are cut off from the celestial world while He is there, for is He not your head? Has He not Himself declared that you are a member of His body, of His flesh, and of His bones? Oh, friend, you are not separated from heaven while Jesus tells you:

> I feel at my heart all thy sighs and thy groans,
> For thou art most near me, my flesh and my hones,

> In all thy distresses, thy Head feels the pain,
> They all are most needful, not one is in vain.

Oh, poor, disconsolate mourner, Christ remembers you every hour. Your sighs are His sighs; your groans are His groans; your prayers are His prayers:

> He in his measure feels afresh,
> What every member bears.

He is crucified when you are crucified; He dies when you die. You live in Him, and He lives in you, and because He lives you shall live also. You shall rise in Him, and you shall sit together in the heavenly places with Him. Oh, never was husband nearer to his wife, never head nearer to the members, and never soul nearer to the body of this flesh than Christ is to you. While it is so, think not that heaven and earth are divided. They are but kindred worlds, two ships moored close to one another, and one short plank of death will enable you to step from one into the other. This ship, all black and coal-like, having done the coasting trade, the dusty business of today, and being full of the blackness of sorrow. And that ship all golden, with its painted pennon flying and its sail all spread, white as the down of the seabird, fair as the angel's wing. I tell you the ship of heaven is moored side by side with the ship of earth. Though this ship may rock and career on stormy winds and tempests, yet the invisible and golden ship of heaven sails by her side never sundered, never divided, always ready, in order that when the hour shall come, you may leap from the black, dark ship and step upon the golden deck of that thrice happy one on which you shall sail forever.

But, O beloved, there are other golden links besides this that bind the present to the future and time to eternity. And what are time and eternity, after all, to the believer, but like the Siamese twins never to be separated? This earth is heaven below, the next world is but a heaven above. It is the same house—this is the lower room, and that the upper, but the same roof covers both and the same dew falls upon each. Remember, beloved, that the spirits of the just made perfect are never far from you and me if we are lovers of Jesus. All those who have passed the flood still have communion with us. Do we not sing:

> The saints on earth, and all the dead,
>   But one communion make;
> All join in Christ, the living Head,
>   And of his grace partake.

We have but one Head for the church triumphant and for the church militant:

> One army of the living God,
> To his command we bow;
> Part of the host have cross'd the flood,
> And part are crossing now.

Does not the apostle tell us that the saints above are a cloud of witnesses? After he had mentioned Abraham, Isaac, Jacob, Gideon, Barak, and Jephthah, did he not say, "Wherefore seeing we also are compassed about with so great a cloud of witnesses, let us lay aside every weight" (Heb. 12:1)? Lo, we are running in the plains and the glorified ones are looking down upon us. Your mother's eyes follow you, young man; a father's eyes are looking down upon you, young woman. The eyes of my godly grandmother, long since glorified, I doubt not, rest on me perpetually. No doubt, in heaven they often talk of us. I think they sometimes visit this poor earth—they never go out of heaven, it is true, for heaven is everywhere to them. This world is to them but just one corner of God's heaven, one shady bower of paradise.

The saints of the living God are, I doubt not, very near to us when we think them very far away. At any rate, they still remember us, still look for us. For this is ever upon their hearts—the truth that they without us cannot be made perfect. They cannot be a perfect church until we are gathered in, and therefore do they long for our appearing.

But, to come to our text a little more minutely, it assures us that the angels have communion with us. Bright spirits, firstborn children of God, do you think of me? Oh, cherubim, great and mighty; seraphim, burning, winged with lightning, do you think of us? Gigantic is your stature. Our poet tells us that the wand of an angel might make a mast for some tall admiral. Doubtless, he was right when he said so. Those angels of God are creatures mighty and strong, doing His commandments, hearkening to His Word. And do they take notice of us? Let the Scripture answer, "Are they not all ministering spirits, sent forth to minister for them who shall be heirs of salvation?" (Heb. 1:14). "The angel of the LORD encampeth round about them that fear him" (Ps. 34:7). "For he shall give his angels charge over thee, to keep thee in all thy ways. They shall bear thee up in their hands, lest thou dash thy foot against a stone" (91:11–12). Yes, the brightest angels are but the serving men of the saints. They are our lacqueys and our footmen. They wait upon us. They are the troops of our bodyguard. We might, if our eyes were opened, see what Elisha saw—horses of fire and chariots of fire round about us—so that we could joyously say, "More are they that are with us than they that are against us."

Our text tells us that the angels of God rejoice over repenting sinners. How is that? They are always as happy as they can be. How can they be any happier? The text does not say that they are any happier but perhaps that they show their happiness more. A man may have a Sabbath every day, as he ought to have if he be a Christian. Yet on the first day of the week he will let his Sabbatism come out plainly, for then the world shall see that he does rest. "A merry heart hath a continual feast" (Prov. 15:15), but then even the merry heart has some special days on which it feasts well. To the glorified every day is a Sabbath, but of some it can be said, "For that sabbath day was an high day" (John 19:31). There are days when the angels sing more loudly than usual. They are always harping well God's praise, but sometimes the gathering hosts who have been flitting far through the universe come home to their center. Around the throne of God, standing in serried ranks and marshaled not for battle but for music, on certain set and appointed days they chant the praises of the Son of God, "[who] hath loved us, and hath given himself for us" (Eph. 5:2). And do you ask me when those days occur? I tell you, the birthday of every Christian is a sonnet day in heaven. There are Christmas days in paradise, where Christ's high mass is kept. And Christ is glorified not because He was born in a manger but because He is born in a broken heart. There are days—good days in heaven, days of sonnet, red-letter days—of overflowing adoration. And these are days when the shepherd brings home the lost sheep upon his shoulder, when the church has swept her house and found the lost piece of money. For then are these friends and neighbors called together, and they rejoice with joy unspeakable and full of glory over one sinner that repents.

I have thus, I hope, shown you that there is a greater connection between earth and heaven than any of us dreamed. And now let none of us think, when we look upward to the blue sky, that we are far from heaven. It is a very little distance from us. When the day comes we shall go posthaste there, even without horses and chariots of fire. Balaam called it a land that is very far off. We know better—it is a land that is very near. Even now:

> By faith we join our hands
> With those that went before,
> And greet the blood-besprinkled bands
> Upon the eternal shore.

All hail, bright spirits! I see you now. All hail, angels! All hail, you who are redeemed! A few more hours or days or months, and we shall join your happy throng. Until then, your joyous fellowship, your sweet compassion shall ever be our comfort and our consolation. And having weathered all storms of life, we shall at last anchor with you within the port of everlasting peace.

The Judgment of the Angels

But the angels are said to sing whenever a sinner repents. Let us see if there is any judgment in their song or whether they make a mistake. Why do angels sing over penitent sinners?

In the first place, I think it is because they remember the days of Creation. You know, when God made this world and fixed the beams of the heavens in sockets of light, the morning stars sang together and the sons of God shouted for joy. As they saw star after star flying abroad like sparks from the great anvil of Omnipotence, they began to sing. Every time they saw a new creature made upon this little earth, they praised afresh. When first they saw light they clapped their hands and said, "Great is Jehovah; for He said 'Light be!' and light was." And when they saw sun and moon and stars, again they clapped their hands, and they said,

> To him that made great lights: for his mercy endureth for ever: The sun to rule by day: for his mercy endureth for ever: The moon and stars to rule by night: for his mercy endureth for ever (Ps. 136:7–9).

And over everything He made, they chanted evermore that sweet song, "Creator, thou art to be magnified; for thy mercy endureth for ever."

Now, when they see a sinner returning, they see the creation over again, for repentance is a new creation. No man ever repents until God makes in him a new heart and a right spirit. I do not know that ever since the day when God made the world, with the exception of new hearts, the angels have seen God make anything else. He may, if He has so pleased, have made fresh worlds since that time. But perhaps the only instance of new creation they have ever seen since the first day is the creation of a new heart and a right spirit within the breast of a poor penitent sinner. Therefore do they sing because creation comes over again.

I doubt not, too, that they sing because they behold God's works afresh shining in excellence. When God first made the world, He said of it, "It was very good" (Gen. 1:31). He could not say so now. There are many of you that God could not say that of. He would have to say the very reverse. He would have to say, "No, that is very bad, for the trail of the serpent has swept away your beauty, and that moral excellence which once dwelt in manhood has passed away." But when the sweet influences of the Spirit bring men to repentance and faith again, God looks upon man and He says, "It is very good." For what His Spirit makes is like Himself—good and holy and precious—and God smiles again over His twice-made creation and says once more, "It is very good." Then the angels begin again and praise His name, whose works are always good and full of beauty.

But, beloved, the angels sing over sinners that repent because they know what that poor sinner has escaped. You and I can never imagine all the depths of hell. Shut out from us by a black veil of darkness, we cannot tell the horrors of that dismal dungeon of lost souls. Happily, the wailings of the damned have never startled us, for a thousand tempests were but a child's whisper compared with one wail of a damned spirit. It is not possible for us to see the tortures of those souls who dwell eternally within an anguish that knows no alleviation. These eyes would become sightless balls of darkness if they were permitted for an instant to look into that ghastly shrine of torment. Hell is horrible, for we may say of it, Eye has not seen, nor ear heard, neither has it entered into the heart of man to conceive the horrors which God has prepared for them that hate Him. But the angels know better than you or I could guess.

They know it. Not that they have felt it, but they remember that day when Satan and his angels rebelled against God. They remember the day when the third part of the stars of heaven revolted against their liege Lord. They have not forgotten how the red right hand of Jehovah Jesus was wrapped in thunder. They do not forget that breach in the battlements of heaven when, down from the greatest heights to the lowest depths, Lucifer and his hosts were hurled. They have never forgotten how, with sound of trumpet, they pursued the flying foe down to the gulfs of black despair. As they neared that place were the great serpent is to be bound in chains, they remember how they saw Tophet, which was prepared of old, the pile whereof is fire and much wood. They recollect how, when they winged back their flight, every tongue was silent, although they might well have shouted the praise of Him who conquered Lucifer. But on them all there did sit a solemn awe of One who could smite a cherubim and cast him in hopeless bonds of everlasting despair. They knew what hell was, for they had looked within its jaws and had seen their own brothers fast enclosed within them. Therefore, when they see a sinner saved, they rejoice because there is one less to be food for the never-dying worm—one more soul escaped out of the mouth of the lion.

There is yet a better reason. The angels know what the joys of heaven are, and, therefore, they rejoice over one sinner that repents. We talk about pearly gates, golden streets, white robes, harps of gold, crowns of amaranth, and all that, but if an angel could speak to us of heaven, he would smile and say, "All these fine things are but child's talk, and you are little children. You cannot understand the greatness of eternal bliss. Therefore, God has given you a child's hornbook and an alphabet in which you may learn the first rough letters of what heaven is. But what it is you do not know. O mortal, your eye has never yet beheld its splendors; your ear has never yet been ravished with its melodies; your heart has never been transported with its peerless joys." You may talk, think, guess, and dream, but you can never measure the infinite heaven that God has provided for His children. Therefore it is, when they see a soul saved and a sinner repenting, that they clap their hands. They know that all those blessed mansions are theirs, since all these sweet places of everlasting happiness are the entail of every sinner that repents.

But I want you just to read the text again, while I dwell upon another thought. "There is joy in the presence of the angels of God over one sinner that repenteth." Now, why do they not save their joy until that sinner dies and goes to heaven? Why do they rejoice over him when he repents? My Arminian friend, I think, ought to go to heaven to set them right upon this matter. According to his theory, it must be very wrong of them, because they rejoice prematurely. According to the Arminian doctrine a man may repent, yet he may be lost. He may have grace to repent and believe, yet he may fall from grace and be a castaway. Now, angels, don't be too fast. Perhaps you may have to repent of this one day. If the Arminian doctrine be true, I would advise you to save your song for greater joys. Why, angels, perhaps the people that you are singing over today you will have to mourn over tomorrow. I am quite sure that Arminius never taught his doctrine in heaven. I do not know whether he is there—I hope he is, but he is no longer an Arminian. But if he ever taught his doctrine there, he would be put out. The reason why angels rejoice is because they know that when a sinner repents, he is absolutely saved, or else they would rejoice prematurely and would have good cause for retracting their merriment on some future occasion. But the angels know what Christ meant when He said, " And I give unto them eternal life; and they shall never perish, neither shall any man pluck them out of my hand" (John 10:28). Therefore they rejoice over repenting sinners because they know they are saved.

There is yet one more fact I will mention before I leave this point. It is said that the angels "rejoice over one sinner that repenteth." Now this evening it shall be my happy privilege to give the right hand of fellowship to no less than forty-eight sinners that have repented. There will be great joy and rejoicing in our churches tonight because these forty-eight have been immersed on a profession of their faith. But how loving are the angels to men, for they rejoice over *one* sinner that repents. There she is, in that garret where the stars look between the tiles. There is a miserable bed in that room with but one bit of covering, and she lies there to die! Poor creature! Many a night she has walked the streets in the time of her merriment, but now her joys are over. A foul disease, like a demon, is devouring her heart! She is dying fast, and no one cares for her soul! But there, in that chamber, she turns her face to the wall and cries, "O You who saved Magdalene, save me. Lord I repent. Have mercy upon me, I beseech You." Did the bells ring in the street? Was the trumpet blown?

Ah! no. Did men rejoice? Was there a sound of thanksgiving in the midst of the great congregation? No; no one heard it, for she died unseen. But stay! There was one standing at her bedside who noted well that tear. It was an angel who had come down from heaven to watch over this stray sheep and mark its return. No sooner was her prayer uttered than he clapped his wings, and there was seen flying up to the pearly gates a spirit like a star. The heavenly guards came crowding to the gate, crying, "What news, O son of fire?"

He said, " ' Tis done."

"And what is done?" they said.

"Why, she has repented."

"What! she who was once a chief of sinners, has she turned to Christ?"

"' Tis even so," said he. And then they told it through the streets, and the bells of heaven rang marriage peals, for Magdalene was saved. She who had been the chief of sinners was turned to the living God.

It was in another place. A poor neglected little boy in ragged clothing had run about the streets for many days. Tutored in crime, he was paving his path to the gallows. But one morning he passed by a humble room where some men and women were sitting together teaching poor ragged children. He stepped in there, a wild Bedouin of the streets. They talked to him, and they told him about a soul and about an eternity—things he had never heard before. They spoke of Jesus and of good tidings of great joy to this poor friendless lad. He went another Sabbath and another, his wild habits hanging about him, for he could not get rid of them. At last it happened that his teacher said to him one day, "Jesus Christ receives sinners." That little boy ran, but not home, for it was but a mockery to call it so—where a drunken father and a lascivious mother kept a hellish riot together. He ran and under some dry arch, or in some wild unfrequented corner, he bent his little knees. There he cried, that poor creature in his rags, "Lord save me, or I perish." The little Arab was on his knees—the little thief was saved! He said: "Jesus, lover of my soul, let me to Thy bosom fly."

And up from that old arch, from that forsaken hovel, there flew a spirit glad to bear the news to heaven that another heir of glory was born to God.

I might picture many such scenes. But will each of you try to picture your own? You remember the occasion when the Lord met with you. Ah! little did you think what a commotion there was in heaven. If the queen had ordered out all her soldiers, the angels of heaven would not have stopped to notice them. If all the princes of earth had marched in pageant through the streets with all their robes and jewelry and crowns and all their regalia, their chariots and their horsemen; if the pomps of ancient monarchies had risen from the tomb; if all the might of Babylon and Tyre and Greece had been concentrated into one great parade, yet not an angel would have stopped in his course to smile at those poor tawdry things. But over you—the vilest of the vile, the poorest of the poor, the most obscure and unknown—over you angelic wings were hovering, and concerning you it was said on earth and sung in heaven, "Hallelujah, for a child is born to God today."

A Lesson for the Saints

And now I must conclude with this lesson to the saints. I think, beloved, it will not be hard for you to learn. The angels of heaven rejoice over sinners that repent. Saints of God, will not you and I do the same? I do not think the church rejoices enough. We all grumble enough and groan enough, but very few of us rejoice enough. When we take a large number into the church it is spoken of as a great mercy. But is the greatness of that mercy appreciated? I will tell you who they are that can most appreciate the conversion of sinners. They are those that are just converted themselves or those that have been great sinners themselves. Those who have been saved themselves from bondage when they see others coming who have so lately worn the chains are so glad that they can well take the tabret, the harp, the pipe, and the psaltery and praise God that there are other prisoners who have been emancipated by grace. But there are others who can do this better still, and they are the parents and relations of those who are saved. You have thanked God many times when you have seen a sinner saved. But, mother, did you not thank Him most when you saw your son converted? Oh! those holy tears. They are not tears—they are God's diamonds—the tears of a mother's joy, when her son confesses his faith in Jesus. Oh! that glad countenance of the wife when she sees her husband, long bestial and drunken, at last made into a man and a Christian! Oh! that look of joy which a young Christian gives when he sees his father converted, who had long oppressed and persecuted him.

I was preaching this week for a young minister, and being anxious to know his character, I spoke of him with apparent coolness to an estimable lady of his congregation. In a very few moments she began to warm in his favor. She said, "You must not say anything against him, sir. If you do, it is because you do not know him."

"Oh," I said, "I knew him long before you did. He is not much, is he?"

"Well," she said, "I must speak well of him, for he has been a blessing to my servants and family."

I went out into the street and saw some men and women standing about, so I said to them, "I must take your minister away."

"If you do," they said, "we will follow you all over the world, if you take away a man who has done so much good to our souls."

After collecting the testimony of fifteen or sixteen witnesses, I said, "If the man gets such witnesses as these, let him go on. The Lord has opened his mouth, and the Devil will never be able to shut it." These are the witnesses we want—men who can sing with the angels because their own households are converted to God. I hope it may be so with all of you. If any of you are yourselves brought to Christ today—for He is willing to receive you—you will go out of this place singing, and the angels will sing with you. There shall be joy in earth and joy in heaven—on earth peace, and glory to God in the highest. The Lord bless you one and all, for Jesus' sake.

Mahanaim: The Two Camps

Alexander Maclaren (1826–1910) was one of Great Britain's most famous preachers. While pastoring the Union Chapel, Manchester (1858–1903), he became known as "the prince of expository preachers." Rarely active in denominational or civic affairs, Maclaren invested his time in studying the Word in the original languages and in sharing its truths with others in sermons that are still models of effective expository preaching. He published a number of books of sermons and climaxed his ministry by publishing his monumental *Expositions of Holy Scripture.*

This message was taken from *Christ in the Heart,* published in 1902 by Funk and Wagnalls.

Alexander Maclaren

8

MAHANAIM: THE TWO CAMPS

And Jacob went on his way, and the angels of God met him. And when Jacob saw them, he said, This is God's host: and he called the name of that place Mahanaim (Genesis 32:1–2).

THIS VISION CAME at a crisis in Jacob's life. He has just left the house of Laban, his father-in-law, where he had lived for many years, and in company with a long caravan, consisting of wives, children, servants, and all his wealth turned into cattle, is journeying back again to Palestine. His road leads him close by the country of Esau. Jacob was no soldier, and he is naturally terrified to meet his justly incensed brother. And so, as he plods along with his defenseless company trailing behind him, and as you may see the Arab caravans streaming over the same uplands today, all at once in the middle of his march a bright-harnessed army of angels meets him. Whether visible to the eye of sense or, as would appear, only to the eye of faith, they *are* visible to this troubled man. And, in a glow of confident joy, he calls the name of that place "Mahanaim," two camps. One camp was the little one of his down here, with the helpless women and children and his own frightened and defenseless self. The other was the great one up there, or rather in shadowy but most real spiritual presence around about him, as a bodyguard making an impregnable wall between him and every foe. We may take some very plain and everlastingly true lessons out of this story.

The Angels of God Meet Us on the Dusty Road of Common Life

"Jacob went on his way, and the angels of God met him." As he was tramping along there over the lonely

85

fields of Edom, with many a thought on his mind and many a fear at his heart—but feeling: "There is the path that I have to walk on"—all at once the air was filled with the soft rustle of angel wings, and the brightness from the flashing armor of the heavenly hosts flamed across his unexpecting eye. And so is it evermore. The true place for us to receive visions of God is in the path of the homely, prosaic duties that He lays upon us. The dusty road is far more likely to be trodden by angel feet than the remote summits of the mountain, where we sometimes would rather go. Many an hour consecrated to devotion has less of the manifest presence of God than is granted to some weary heart in its commonplace struggle with the little troubles and trials of daily life. These make the doors, as it were, by which the visitants draw near to us.

It is the common duties—"the narrow round, the daily task"—that not only give us "all we ought to ask," but are the selected means and channels by which God's visitants draw near to us. The man that has never seen an angel standing beside him and driving his loom for him or helping him at his counter and his desk and the woman that has never seen an angel—according to the bold realism and homely vision of the old German picture—working with her in the kitchen and preparing the meal for the household have little chance of meeting such visitants at any other point of their experience or event of their lives.

If the week be empty of the angels, you will never catch sight of a feather of their wings on Sunday. And if we do not recognize their presence in the midst of all the prose—and the commonplace and the vulgarity and the triviality and the monotony, the dust of the small duties—we shall go up to the summit of Sinai itself and see nothing there but cold gray stone and everlasting snows. "Jacob went on his way, and the angels of God met him." The true field for religion is the field of common life.

And then another side of the same thought is this, that it is in the path where God has bade us walk that we shall find the angels around us. We may meet them, indeed, on paths of our own choosing, but it will be the sort of angel that Balaam met, with a sword in his hand, mighty and beautiful, but wrathful, too. We had better not front him! But the friendly helpers, the emissaries of God's love, the apostles of His grace do not haunt the roads that we make for ourselves. They confine themselves rigidly to the paths in which God has "before ordained that we should walk in them" (Eph. 2:10). A man has no right to expect, and he will not get, blessing and help and divine gifts when, self-willedly, he has taken the bit between his teeth and is choosing his own road in the world. But if he will say, "Lord! here I am. Put me where You will, and do with me what You will," then he may be sure that that path—though it may be solitary of human companionship and leading up among barren rocks and over bare moorlands, where the sun beats down fiercely—will not be unvisited by a better presence. Then in sweet consciousness of sufficiency of rich grace he shall be able to say, "I being in the way, the LORD led me" (Gen. 24:27).

The Angels of God Meet Us
Punctually at the Hour of Need

Jacob is drawing nearer and nearer to his fear every step. He is now just on the borders of Esau's country and close upon opening communications with his brother. At that critical moment, just before the finger of the clock has reached the point on the dial at which the bell would strike, the needed help comes—the angel guards draw near and camp beside him. It is always so. "God shall help her, and that right early" (Ps. 46:5). His hosts come no sooner and no later than we need. If they appeared before we had realized our danger and our defenselessness, our hearts would not leap up at their coming, as men in a beleaguered town do when the guns of the relieving force are heard booming from afar. Often God's delays seem to us inexplicable and our prayers to have no more effect than if they were spoken to a sleeping Baal. But such delays are merciful. They help us to the consciousness of our need. They let us feel the presence of the sorrow. They give opportunity of proving the weakness of all other supports. They test and increase desire for His help. They throw us more unreservedly into His arms. They afford room for the sorrow or the burden to work its peaceable fruits. So, and in many other ways, delay of succor fits us to receive succor, and our God makes no tarrying but for our sakes.

It is His way to let us come almost to the edge of the precipice, and then, in the very nick of time when another minute and we are over, to stretch out His strong right hand and save us. So Peter is left in prison, though prayer is going up unceasingly for him—and no answer comes. The days of the Passover feast slip away, and still he is in prison and prayer does nothing for him. The last day of his life, according to Herod's purpose, dawns and all the day the church lifts up its voice—but apparently there is no answer nor any that regarded. The night comes and still the vain cry goes up, and heaven seems deaf or apathetic. The night wears on and still no help comes. But in the last watch of that last night when day is almost dawning—at nearly the last minute when escape would have been possible—the angel touches the sleeping apostle and with leisurely calmness, as sure that he had ample time, leads him out to freedom and safety. It was precisely because Jesus loved the household at Bethany that, after receiving the sisters' message, He abode still for two days in the same place where He was. However our impatience may wonder and our faithlessness venture sometimes almost to rebuke Him, when He comes, with words like Mary's and Martha's—"Lord, if thou hadst been here" (John 11:21), such and such sorrows would not have happened, and You could so easily have been here—we should learn the lesson that even if He has delayed so long that the dreaded blow has fallen, He has come soon enough to make it the occasion for a still more glorious communication of His power.

Rest in the Lord, wait patiently for Him, and He shall give you the desires of your heart.

The Angels of God Come
in the Shape We Need

Jacob's want at the moment was protection. Therefore the angels appear in warlike guise and present before the defenseless man another camp, in which he and his unwieldy caravan of women and children and cattle may find security. If his special want had been of some blessing of another kind, no doubt another form of appearance suited with precision to his need would have been imposed upon these angel helpers. For God's gifts to us change their characters, as the rabbis fabled that the manna tasted to each man what each most desired. The same pure heavenly bread has the varying savor that commends it to varying palates. God's grace is protean. It takes all the forms that man's necessities require. As water assumes the shape of any vessel into which it is put, so this great blessing comes to each of us, molded according to the pressure and taking the form of our circumstances and necessities. His fullness is all-sufficient. It is the same blood that, passing to all the members, ministers to each according to the needs and fashion of each. And it is the same grace which, passing to our souls, in each man is shaped according to his present condition and ministers to his present wants.

So, dear friends, in that great fullness each of us may have the thing that we need. The angel who to one man is protection to another shall be teaching and inspiration, to another shall appear with chariots of fire and horses of fire to sweep the rapt soul heavenward. Yet, to another, the angel shall draw near as a deliverer from his fetters, at whose touch the bonds shall fall from off him. To another the angel shall appear as the instructor in duty and the appointer of a path of service, like that vision that shone in the castle to the apostle Paul and said, "As thou hast testified of me in Jerusalem, so must thou bear witness also at Rome" (Acts 23:11). Still, the angel shall appear to another as opening the door of heaven and letting a flood of light come down upon his darkened heart, as to the apocalyptic seer in his rocky

Patmos. And all this works that one and the selfsame Lord of angels, dividing to every man severally as He will and as the man needs. The defenseless Jacob has the manifestation of the divine presence in the guise of armed warriors that guard his unwarlike camp.

I add one last word. Long centuries after Jacob's experience at Mahanaim, another trembling fugitive found himself there, like Jacob, fearful of the vengeance and anger of one who was knit to him by blood. When poor King David was flying from the face of Absalom, his son, the first place where he made a stand and where he remained during the whole of the rebellion was this town of Mahanaim, away on the eastern side of the Jordan. Do you not think that to the kingly exile, in his feebleness and his fear, the very name of his resting place would be an omen? Would he not recall the old story and think to himself of how around that other frightened man "bright-harnessed angels stood in order serviceable." Would he not, as he looked on his little band of friends, faithful among the faithless, have his eyesight cleared to behold the other camp? Such a vision, no doubt, inspired the calm confidence of the psalm that evidently belongs to that dark hour of his life. It made it possible for the hunted, solitary king, with his feeble band, to sing even then, "I will both lay me down in peace, and sleep: for thou, LORD, only makest me dwell in safety" (Ps. 4:8).

Nor is the vision emptied of its power to stay and make brave by all the ages that have passed. The vision was for a moment; the fact is forever. The sun's rays were flashed back from celestial armor, "the next all unreflected shone" on the lonely wastes of the desert— but the host of God was there still. The transitory appearance of the permanent realities is a revelation to us as truly as to the patriarch. Though no angel wings may winnow the air around our road nor any sworded seraphim be seen on our commonplace march, we too have all the armies of heaven with us, if we tread the path that God has marked out and in our weakness and trembling commit ourselves to Him. The heavenly warriors die not and hover around us today, excelling in the strength of their immortal youth. They are as ready to succor us as they were all these centuries ago to guard the solitary Jacob.

Better still, the "captain of the host of the LORD [has] now come" (Josh. 5:14) to be our defense. Our faith has not only to behold the many ministering spirits sent forth to minister to us, but One mightier than they, whose commands they all obey and who Himself is the companion of our solitude and the shield of our defenselessness. It was blessed that Jacob should be met by the many angels of God. It is infinitely more blessed that "*the* angel of the LORD"—the One who is more than the many— "encampeth round about them that fear him, and delivereth them" (Ps. 34:7, emphasis added).

The postscript of the last letter that Gordon sent from Khartoum closed with the words, "The hosts are with me—Mahanaim." Were they not, even though death was near? Was that sublime faith a mistake—the vision an optical delusion? No, for their ranks are arrayed around God's children to keep them from all evil while He wills that they should live, and their chariots of fire and horses of fire are sent to bear them to heaven when He wills that they should die.

The Nature of Angels

Alexander Whyte (1836–1921) was known as "the last of the Puritans," and certainly his sermons were surgical as he magnified the glory of God and exposed the sinfulness of sin. He succeeded the noted Robert S. Candlish as pastor of Free Saint George's and reigned from that influential Edinburgh pulpit for nearly forty years. He loved to "dig again in the old wells" and share with his people truths learned from the devotional masters of the past. His evening Bible courses attracted the young people and led many into a deeper walk with God.

This sermon was taken from *The Treasury of Alexander Whyte,* edited by Ralph Turnbull and published in 1953 by Fleming H. Revell.

Alexander Whyte

9

THE NATURE OF ANGELS

He took not on him the nature of angels (Hebrews 2:16).

For unto the angels hath he not put in subjection the world to come, whereof we speak. But one in a certain place testified, saying, What is man, that thou art mindful of him? or the son of man, that thou visitest him? Thou madest him a little lower than the angels; thou crownedst him with glory and honour, and didst set him over the works of thy hands: Thou hast put all things in subjection under his feet. For in that he put all in subjection under him, he left nothing that is not put under him. But now we see not yet all things put under him. But we see Jesus, who was made a little lower than the angels for the suffering of death, crowned with glory and honour; that he by the grace of God should taste death for every man (Hebrews 2:5–9).

Being made so much better than the angels, as he hath by inheritance obtained a more excellent name than they (Hebrews 1:4).

WHY IS SO much made of the angels in these passages? Why is there so much space and quotation and argument expended on what seems to us a somewhat irrelevant matter? Might not the Epistle to the Hebrews have been greatly condensed and simplified had the reader's attention been fixed at once on the priesthood of Christ instead of having to pass through this long introduction concerning angels and Moses, which no one disputes and which seems not to bring any strength to the great argument of the epistle?

A slight reading of the book will suffice to start these questions, but it requires a deeper and harder reading fitly to answer them. And still such a reading will be amply repaid in a more living and intelligent hold of the main theme when we come to it.

The introductory portion of this epistle is not addressed

to mature and well-grounded Christians of the nineteenth century so much as to the immature Jewish converts of the first, who were as yet "unskilful in the word of righteousness" (5:13) and had need of milk and not of strong meat. They had not yet understood the principles of the doctrine of baptism and laying on of hands, about Moses and the Law, and about angels and their place in its dispensation. The apostle had to become all things to all men. He knew that there was simply no use plunging at once into the heart of his theme when such obstacles as these lay in the way of his readers following him. Hence he spends several chapters on clearing the path for the weaker brothers and sisters, who feared that in going forward with the great Christian movement they were thereby somehow in danger of forsaking the old paths in which their fathers had walked.

But still the question awaits an answer. Why so much in the first and second chapters concerning angels?

The answer is simply this: the appearances and messages of angels held the place in the Old Testament that the appearance and teaching of Christ do in the New. A light surrender of the old order and the ministry of angels would have revealed but a poor capacity for receiving the new. These Hebrews—with the blood of Abraham and Isaac and Jacob, of Moses and the prophets in their veins—would have their childhood steeped in Old Testament narrative concerning the deliverances wrought and the comfort sent by angels, for all down the nation's checkered history their cheering words had been heard and their ministering wings seen. And, above all, the angel of the covenant, the angel of the Lord, had brought God the Father so near that it might almost be said that they had in him preludes and anticipations of the incarnation itself. It was through his ministry that the patriarchs were called and led and prospered. It was through his disposition of the Law that it came into Moses' hands. It was through him that the prophets spoke to the fathers. God took the form, and came in the character, of an angel when He conveyed anything new or confirmed any old revelation of grace or truth to the Hebrew people.

In a word, what the Son is under the New Testament economy, that the ministry of angels was under the Old.

But retrograde and Judaizing teachers had played on the prejudices and the piety of the Hebrew Christians by culting Moses and the Law that came by the dispensation of angels. Therefore, to show that Jesus is rightly counted of more honor than Moses and that He has by indisputable inheritance a greater than an angelic name, Paul has undertaken to show that Christ has superseded the ministry of angels in revealing the Father and also has set aside the stewardship of Moses, being a Son over His own house.

We are now ready to follow the apostle into this argumentative passage of chapter 1, in which he seeks to exalt the dignity of Christ above the angels.

Verse 3 dwells, in several striking clauses, on what the Son was and is and in His divine nature will ever be—the "brightness of [the Father's] glory, and the express image of his person, and upholding all things by the word of his power." Then comes a clause covering His work on earth: "by himself [he] purged our sins." And then another clause comes stating that He is now "on the right hand of the Majesty on high."

Verse 4, then, accounts for His exaltation and so carries forward the arguments for this excellent dignity of the risen Redeemer. He has sat down at the right hand of God, "being made so much better than the angels, as he hath by inheritance obtained a more excellent name than they."

This passage was one of the Arian strongholds during the great controversy concerning the eternal sonship and perfect divinity of the Redeemer. This verse was taken along with the second verse of the third chapter, in which it is said that Christ was "faithful to him that appointed [or made] him"; also, Acts 2:36, in which Peter says: "Therefore let all the house of Israel know assuredly, that God hath made that same Jesus, whom ye have crucified, both Lord and Christ." In those passages, as here, the word "made" plainly occurs concerning the Savior. And that fact kept these verses like so many disputed provinces that were taken and retaken by Arian and orthodox, until Athanasius finally settled the sense of these texts and put into the great creed that the Son was "begotten not made." But how did he and his followers get over the plain words of the text? How is the Arian sound shown to contain an orthodox sense?

In this way and from the plain text of Scripture. The Son who was in the form of God, or, as here, the "express image of his person," and who "thought it not robbery to be equal with God: but made himself of no reputation, and took upon him the form of a servant" (Phil. 2:6–7). The Maker of all was made in the likeness of men, being "made of a woman, made under the law" (Gal. 4:4). "And being found in fashion as a man, he humbled himself, and became obedient unto death, even the death of the cross. Wherefore God also hath highly exalted him, and given him a name which is above every name" (Phil. 2:8–9), a more excellent name than angel ever bore. "That at the name of Jesus every knee should bow . . . and that every tongue should confess that Jesus Christ is Lord, to the glory of God the Father" (vv. 10–11).

The Arians understood not His generation. Because He was "found in fashion as a man," His eternal life was denied. They staggered at the grace of the Incarnation. The mystery of godliness, God manifest in the flesh, was too deep for them. For remaining what He was, the eternal Son, He became what He was not, the Son of Man and of the seed of Abraham. In being made man, He "was made a little lower than the angels." Those spiritual beings whom He created by His own power actually came and ministered to Him after His temptation in the wilderness and strengthened Him in His agony in the Garden. But though He has thus emptied Himself, though He has thus for our salvation become what He was not, still He necessarily remains what He was, Son of God. Conditions change, relations hold. He is Son of God made Son of Man; He is Son still, though Son incarnate and in a temporary state of suffering and emptiness and humiliation. Here, then, is a condition of things that makes it plain why Scripture should fearlessly say about its divine Lord that He was made Lord and Christ, having been "faithful to him that appointed him"; that having finished His work the Father raised Him from the dead, gave Him back His glory, and made Him so much higher than the angels, as He originally and prior to His humiliation had a much more excellent name than they.

At the resurrection and exaltation of Christ He was but putting on again that glory He had, for our service, put off. When He sat down on the right hand of God He was but repossessing Himself of a place and an honor that were inalienably and eternally His own.

But there is more room still for the correct phrase, "made so much better than the angels." For it is not only the Son resuming His suspended honor and returning to His sonship seat, but He is returning in a new character and in a form that shows the Father's grace to be as great in the exaltation of Christ as the Son's grace was shown to be great in His voluntary humiliation. For the Son is returning to the Father's throne, the Father's bosom, not only divine Son still, but Son of Man in addition. It is a new honor and experience to the Son, and a new display of grace is to realize that He should reenter to the most excellent glory as a man. It is true that the assumption of the human nature into the divine glory in heaven was an easy and a natural thing after its assumption into the sonship on earth, that it drew the rest naturally, necessarily after it. Hence this is no empty apotheosis of a man but a far more wonderful and gracious work, the incarnation of the Son of God and His subsequent reinstallation into all the sonship rights and prerogatives. He took our nature, in it purged our sins, and then returned whence He had come, went back to the Father with whom He had been before the world was. Thus the exaltation is not of the divine nature only, nor is it a deification of the human only. It is the exaltation of that divine person who is now God-Man. It is the answer to the Son's prayer, "Glorify thou me with thine own self with the glory which I had with thee before the world was" (John 17:5)—before I had emptied myself that I might glorify You.

It was a new thing on the earth that the eternal Son of God should tabernacle among men, purging their sins; it was a new thing in heaven that a son of man should appear at the right hand of the Majesty on high. For this man whom the Jews crucified is assuredly now made Lord Christ. And He is as high above angels as a lord is above his dependents, as the son is above the servants. And they are ever confessing it. When He had finished the work that was given Him to do—when He had purged our sins, burst the bonds of death, blessed His disciples, and sent them to wait on the Spirit's descent—earth had no more work for Him to do. And He turned His face to His Father's house. That hour there rang a shout through heaven, the like of which had not been heard there since the morning stars sang together—the sons of God shouted for joy at the creating work of the eternal Son.

"Lift up your heads, O ye gates; and be ye lift up, ye everlasting doors; and the King of glory shall come in" (Ps. 24:7)! And as the Son passed in and ascended to His Father's presence, the angels looking on might have said, "He is preferred before us, for He was before us." They had wondered at His surpassing grace when He had passed out into this dark and sinful world; they worshiped afresh as He passed in again, the Redeemer and Brother of fallen men.

Thus He who had so lately stood in Pilate's judgment hall with a scarlet rag on His shoulders, a crown of thorns on His head, a reed in His hand, and a crowd of rude men paying Him mock homage until the hour should come to crucify Him, now compels the deep worship of the highest heavens as He enters with glory as the Lamb that has been slain, having on His vesture and on His thigh a name written more excellent than that of any angel—King of Kings and Lord of Lords (Rev. 19:16).

And a voice was heard in heaven saying, "Sit thou at my right hand, until I make thine enemies thy footstool" (Ps. 110:1). "Thy throne . . . is for ever and ever" (45:6; Heb. 1:8). "Ask of me, and I shall give thee the heathen for thine inheritance, and the uttermost parts of the earth for thy possession" (Ps. 2:8). "And let all the angels of God worship him" (Heb. 1:6) and wait on his will.

In this marvelous way the eternal Son was "made so much better than the angels, as he hath by inheritance obtained a much more excellent name than they."

But the apostle cannot set all this as yet before his Hebrew readers. He has to walk as they are able to follow. He has to argue on premises they already accept and quote proof and illustration from the Book they read and reverence. Hence he hitches himself to the Old Testament and goes to work to prove by lengthened and full quotation that the Messiah promised there, the Messiah promised to and expected by the fathers, was one who confessedly had a more excellent name than the angels or than Moses. The prophecy that came by the mouth of angels gave to the coming One a name and work far higher than their own. They came and spoke as witnesses and heralds of a greater than any prophet or king who had yet arisen.

Now, the Hebrew Christians confessed that Jesus was the Messiah, that all the messianic promises and expectations were fulfilled, or were yet to be fulfilled, in Him. And the apostle, to disarm their doubt and allay their discomfort about the place the old was getting in the triumph of the new, shows them that the new is the triumph of the old, that Jesus who is the Messiah has simply gotten that which was promised to the Messiah; that His name and rank are higher than the angels that it might be fulfilled that was spoken by Moses and the Fathers and in the Prophets concerning Him. "Come, open your Scriptures," he says, "and I will show you that that Old Testament—book and economy—you are so jealous for gives such a name and place to the Messiah as my doctrine gives to Him whom you confess to be the Messiah."

Hence the long quotations that fill the page and lay a deep and broad messianic foundation for this weighty epistle. But the method of proof that an inspired writer drew out to satisfy the mind and settle the heart of an ancient Christian fails, it seems, to satisfy and settle the modern rationalist. The apostle's exegesis yields dogmatic results that are distasteful and inadmissible; therefore his scholarship, his intelligence, his inspiration, and even his literary honesty are boldly questioned and impugned. And the narrow, irrational canon is laid down, even by theological teachers, that we are to "read Scripture and quote it like any other book."

If this is admitted, of course there is an end, if not of religious sentiment and moral duty, at least of all defined and trustworthy theology, as well as of much of the peculiar edification and comfort obtained from Holy Scripture. The believer and the rationalist thus part company at the very threshold of the question. The Christian cannot read Scripture as he reads another book because for him no other book can claim such an author, as no other book raises such questions or claims or commands such a hearing. As the Book itself says: "The letter killeth, but the spirit giveth life" (2 Cor. 3:6). A literal, rationalistic interpretation kills all life out of the Psalms and Prophets, just as a devout and spiritual reading gets life and gives it.

Many questions connected with the principles on which New Testament writers quote from and allude to the Old are raised and discussed in view of this passage before us. But they are more suited to the study and the classroom than to the pulpit. Still, before looking at these quotations in passing, it may be useful to some to say a word on the general relation that holds between the first volume of Holy Scripture and the second, between the Psalms and Prophets on the one hand and the Gospels and Epistles on the other.

There is nothing in the literary history of the world at all to compare with the Bible, viewed purely on its literary side. A succession of writers has arisen for many generations of men and in lands far separated in place and circumstance from each other and produced a book with beginning, middle, and end—a book that is one in plan and doctrine, and aim and spirit, though it deals with the most difficult and lofty questions and though scholars and poets and orators, craftsmen and fishermen and plowmen have contributed to its contents. Take it at the close of any of its divisions—at the close of the Pentateuch, at the close of the Psalms, at the close of the Prophets—the Book is complete, as a seed or a bud is complete. It is perfect for its stage, but its stage is one of growth and maturity.

Read Moses and the Prophets and you cannot fail to see that the Old Testament is one in this, that whoever is the writer or the speaker, the spirit of the book, the attitude of the religious life, is one of expectancy in outlook.

The old stands ever on tiptoe looking for the rising of the new, holding forth empty hands—empty but for the typical washing they celebrate and the prophetic words they hold. They rejoice in God and in what He has done, but they feel that His best waits to be done. They rejoice with the chastened joy of sojourners and strangers who feel that without us they are not to be made perfect. On one page the prophet is so lifted up in hope and faith that a thousand years are as one day. He seems to see the Day of the Lord and his hope is made glad. Turn it and a day of sorrow has fallen, and he is crying, "How long, O Lord, how long?"

The messianic prophecies are like the garden of the Lord, but it is early summer there. It is rich with buds and blossoms. It is not yet the time of fruit bearing. The day of the Lord comes and the buds burst in His presence. The fullness of time has brought the fulfilling of prophecy and the unlocking of the type. And still the Book must be read according to its own laws and not as another book. Even when prophecy is fulfilled and the antitype has come, still He is found to speak another language than the wise men and princes of this world know. He still speaks in words that the Holy Spirit teaches, which are to one man foolishness, to another the wisdom of God, because by Him they were spiritually discovered. "Open thou mine eyes, that I may behold wondrous things out of thy law" (Ps. 119:18).

The New Testament preacher or writer may be not unfitly likened to a man thinking or writing in a language he is both learning and adding to as he writes. In the construction of an argument like this the apostle is like one seeking a fit word to clothe his thought so as to place both before his readers. Yes, the thought will not shape itself aright until the right word comes—until the old figure and illustration are found that at once embody it fully and shed light on it clearly. As he recalls and sets down in order those quotations, he knows that they will set forth with authority as well as perspicacity what is struggling in his mind. This habit of leaning on the past and drawing strength from it, even when they were going far beyond it, is as characteristic of the prophets as it is of the apostles. David and Isaiah are the scholars of Moses. They quote from, expound, and apply him just as our apostle here quotes and applies them. And the books then appear as at once grafted on and growths out of one another.

To change the figure, the rich, golden threads of messianic prophecy are visible from the beginning of the web, though they do not find their end and design until the figure rises in the middle of the work into which they enter, to be lost in its wealth and beauty. And the apostle here but traces some of the brightest and strongest of such threads up through the loom to prove that the original design had contemplated and made provision for such a central figure.

He is but in his way doing what Christ Himself did when teaching the reluctant disciples concerning the old intention of His suffering and His glory. "These are the words which I spake unto you, while I was yet with you, that all things must be fulfilled, which were written in the law of Moses, and in the prophets, and in the psalms, concerning me" (Luke 24:44). Thus opened he the understanding of the Hebrew Christians to both the messiahship and the sonship of Jesus. For He who was eternal Son, when He had purged our sins, sat down again at the right hand of God, being made so much better than the angels as He has by inheritance, and even by Jewish prophecy, a much more excellent name than they. "For," he goes on to quote from the Hebrew Scriptures, "unto which of the angels said [the Father] at any time, Thou art my son, this day have I begotten thee?" (Heb. 1:5). Now, He said this to the Messiah in prophecy.

"And again, when he bringeth in the firstbegotten into the world, he saith, And let all the angels of God worship him. And of the angels he saith, Who maketh his angels spirits, and his ministers a flame of fire" (vv. 6–7). And, again, quoting from the great messianic psalms, the apostle proves that the coming One is then addressed as possessing just such royal dignity and state as Jesus is now advanced to. Indeed, we search in vain in the historical and doctrinal books of the New Testament for a richer and more exact statement of the Son's glory and reward than we find here in a prophetic psalm concerning the Messiah. "Thy throne, O God, is for ever and ever: a sceptre of righteousness is the sceptre of thy kingdom. Thou hast loved righteousness, and hated iniquity; therefore God, even thy God, hath anointed thee with oil of gladness above thy fellows" (vv. 8–9).

The psalm from which the apostle quotes next is not usually looked on as properly a messianic psalm. But he finds language there that he knows his readers must admit to be applicable to the Son, as he and they are at one that the Son created the worlds: "Thou, Lord, in the beginning hast laid the foundation of the earth; and the heavens are the works of thine hands: they shall perish; but thou remainest; and they all shall wax old as doth a garment; and as a vesture shalt thou fold them up, and they shall be changed: but thou art the same, and thy years shall not fail" (vv. 10–12).

In a word, to come back to the original thought: To which of the angels has the Father said at any time, Sit on my right hand until I make thine enemies thy footstool? The question more than answers itself, for, confessedly, the angels are but ministering spirits sent forth from the Son's throne to minister to those He has redeemed, to those who are to be heirs of salvation.

Of this argument and proof, this, then, is the sum: He is Son, in His incarnation and exalted state, Son of God, and angels are His ministers and messengers.

By these quotations and references the apostle proves what he has advanced above, that the Son is higher than the highest of creatures, better by so much as His inherited name was better than theirs. He is Son and heir; they are servants and ministers of His.

But His name has an excellency above that of inheritance. He inherits a great name from His Father, but He adds fresh glory to His name as the ages roll on.

He is Son by nature, but He is creator and redeemer. He is the Messiah of the Old Testament and the Jesus of the New, a sacrifice on earth and a great high priest in heaven. By grace He has won those names as by His sword alone and added them to that of Son. But that original, inherited name is the ground and basis of all, just as His divine nature underlies His human and all that in it He performs. He went forth as Son to make all things; He was set forth as Son to inherit man. As Son of God He came forth from the Father to be the brightness of His glory and the express image of His person, and as Son of God and Son of Man He himself purged our sins. But in all these He got Him glory. Now He has a name written so full, so deep, so rich with gracious significance that hitherto no man knows it but He Himself. But that rich name He now bears will be opened up and put on the lips of His people when they are finally with Him to behold His eternal glory as Son and His added glory as Savior. But, in the meantime, His excellent name grows as His work grows and as His heirship falls in, as in our names a new syllable added may be to the initiated a hint of a whole family history. An ancestry of wealth and honor may be claimed and conceded, and a rich inheritance held by a few letters added to a personal name. Thus ancient names are not seldom made up of fragments of history. They are badges of rank and signs of heirship and possession. Thus it is that when He shall in heaven or on earth have finished the work His Father and His brothers have given Him to do, He is to be brought forth to the eyes of His people. He is to be greeted by the names Faithful and True, not indeed for the first time, but for the first time in all their fullness and warmth on our lips. On His head shall be many crowns, and He shall have a name written that no man has hitherto known but He Himself:

> Jesus, my Lord! I know His name,
> His name is all my boast:
> Nor will He put my soul to shame,
> Nor let my hope be lost.
> Then will He own His servant's name
> Before His Father's face,
> And in the New Jerusalem
> Appoint my soul a place.

The full knowledge of His name is too wonderful for you. The deep things hidden in it are past finding out. Your heart loses the awful thrill that runs through it as you hear that He is the brightness of His Father's glory and the express image of His person. But surely your sin and need will not let you forget what the angel of the Lord said to Joseph: "Thou shalt call his name Jesus: for he shall save his people from their sins" (Matt. 1:21).

Angelic Studies

Charles Haddon Spurgeon (1834–1892) is undoubtedly the most famous minister of the nineteenth century. Converted in 1850, he united with the Baptists and soon began to preach in various places. He became pastor of the Baptist church in Waterbeach, England, in 1851, and three years later he was called to the decaying Park Street Church, London. Within a short time the work began to prosper, a new church was built and dedicated in 1861, and Spurgeon became London's most popular preacher. In 1855, he began to publish his sermons weekly; today they make up the fifty-seven volumes of *The Metropolitan Tabernacle Pulpit*. He founded a pastor's college and several orphanages.

This sermon was taken from *The Metropolitan Tabernacle Pulpit,* volume 16.

Charles Haddon Spurgeon

10

ANGELIC STUDIES

To the intent that now unto the principalities and powers in heavenly places might be known by the church the manifold wisdom of God (Ephesians 3:10).

THE "principalities and powers in heavenly places" to whom the apostle here refers are, no doubt, the angels. These bright and glorious spirits, never having fallen into sin, did not need to be redeemed; therefore, in the sense of being cleansed from guilt, they have no share in the atoning sacrifice of Christ. Yet it is interesting to notice how our Lord did, as it were, pass and repass their shining ranks when He sped His way down to the regions of death and when He came back triumphant to the realms of glory. Thus in one place "we see Jesus . . . *made a little lower than the angels* for the suffering of death" (Heb. 2:9, emphasis added). In another place we learn that the Father "raised him from the dead, and set him at his own right hand in the heavenly places, *far above all principality, and power, and might, and dominion*" (Eph. 1:20–21, emphasis added). It is possible that the mediation of Christ has a bearing upon them and has henceforth confirmed them in their holiness, so that by no means shall they ever be tempted or led into sin in the future. It may be so. But this much seems to be evident, that though they had no direct share in redemption, they feel nevertheless an interest in it and are to be instructed by its results.

The sublime plan of the Gospel of the grace of God, which is so entirely beyond the compass of our natural faculties that we could never by searching have found it out, appears to have been equally beyond the grasp of angelic intelligence—a mystery that excited their wistful inquiry. But by the church (that is to say, by the divine

107

counsel and conduct in forming and perfecting the church) there is made known to them the manifold wisdom of God as they have never learned it before. They have kept their first estate and have been obedient to God's behests. They delight to be known as the servants of God, doing His commandments and hearkening to the voice of His Word. They are appointed to exercise some sort of power over various parts of God's creation, hence they are called "principalities and powers." Certainly they are engaged in hymning Jehovah's praise. Much of the music that rises up before His throne comes from the harps of spirits, pure and immaculate, who have never known sin. Yet, though they are thus pure, thus engaged in worship, of such eminent rank in the universe of God, they are never represented as indifferent spectators of anything that our mortal race can do or suffer, but their sympathy with men is constant. Do they not watch over the saints? Is it not written that they "encamp round about them that fear [the LORD]" (Ps. 34:7)? Are they not charged to take care of the saints, to bear them up in their hands, lest they dash their feet against the stones?

Angels, we know, have often been messengers of God's will to the sons of men. They have never shown any reluctance. On the contrary, great has been their joy to bear God's tidings down from heaven to earth. Their sympathy even with fallen men, with men who have grievously sinned and gone astray, is shown by the fact that they rejoice "over one sinner that repenteth, more than over ninety and nine just persons, which need no repentance" (Luke 15:7). They are, as it were, in yonder gilded vessel untossed of tempest, but they have sympathy with us in this poor heavy-laden bark, tossed with tempest and not comforted. I see them there on yonder sea of glass mingled with fire. I hear their harpings, as incessantly their joy goes up in music to the throne of the Most High. But they do not look down with scorn on us poor denizens of this dusky planet. On the contrary, they delight to think of us as their brothers and sisters, as their fellow servants. It will be the consummation of their happiness when we shall all be gathered to the church of the firstborn and that they shall make up the innumerable company of angels that surround the blood-washed throng.

The subject of our meditation, which will be brief, resolves itself into a question: How do angels see the manifold wisdom of God?

How Do Angels Come to See the Manifold Wisdom of God?

In creation. Who can doubt that the angels had seen much of the wisdom of God in creation? With faculties keener and more elevated than ours, faculties that have never been blunted by sin, they can perceive the various contrivances of God's skill both in the animate and the inanimate world. Doubtless as each new star has been minted by God, as each planet has been struck off like a spark from the everlasting anvil, angels, those sons of the morning, have lifted up their songs and have poured forth their plans of joy and gladness. They have seen the wisdom of God in the greatness of creation. In every sphere they have been able to perceive it, for their vision is far more comprehensive than ours. And they have also, no doubt, seen that wisdom in all its minuteness, as manifest in the delicate structure of organized beings. They have also seen that wisdom in the skillful economy of the operations of creative power, for there again they are able with the singleness and certainty of superior optics to perceive what only after long years we have been able to discover, and that by reasoning from the ingenuity of the works to the excellence of the design. What a scale of survey must a seraph have! How readily can we imagine an eye that takes in at once the landscape of the world! He need not confine himself to one single spot in God's universe, but with rapid wings he can steer far and wide over the infinity of space. May he not pause here a moment and there a moment and with a glance peer into the multiform wisdom of God in all the ten thousand thousand worlds that stud the realms of space? Yet with all that facility of observation, it seems that the angels have some parts of the wisdom of God to learn and some lessons of heavenly science to study that creation cannot unfold to their view, to be ascertained and certified by them only through the transcendent work of redemption which the Lord has carried on in His church.

In the Law. Fix your attention for a moment on the word "now" as it is used in the text. On that word, it seems to me, much of the meaning hangs. Long before our Lord came into the world, God had been pleased to reveal somewhat of the wisdom of His grace in the types of the old law. These were full of significance, but at the same time not free from perplexity to the minds of most men. They appear not to have been very intelligible even to the angels, for they are pictured as standing over the mercy seat with wings outspread looking down upon its golden lid anxiously inquiring but not clearly discovering the secret of the old covenant dispensation. Peter says, I suppose in allusion to this, "which things the angels desire to look into" (1 Peter 1:12). But Paul here vehemently sets forth the yearnings of his heart in the exercise of his ministry "to make all men see what is the fellowship of the mystery, which from the beginning of the world hath been hid in God, who created all things by Jesus Christ: to the intent that *now* unto the principalities and powers in heavenly places might be known by the church the manifold wisdom of God" (Eph. 3:9–10, emphasis added). May we not infer from this that though angels saw Moses and Aaron and the long succession of priests that followed them, though they doubtless mingled invisibly in the solemn gatherings that went up to Mount Zion and heard the chantings of the glorious psalms, though they saw the streams of blood that flowed at the altar of burnt offering and marked the rising clouds of smoke that went up from the altar of incense that was in the Holy Place before the Lord, they had not as yet discovered the wisdom of God in its fullness and clearness—the spotless mirror of His power, the reflex image of His glorious perfection? May we also not infer that it must have remained for them to learn it from the church? Since Christ has come, angels are to be students of the manifold wisdom of God as revealed in His work toward His people, preparing them for that grand climax—the espousal of the church and the marriage of the Lamb.

To come closer to the matter we must trace it progressively, as though it were step by step that the angels pursued their study and acquired an insight into this manifold wisdom. It may be they do so. Certainly among the children of men there is much pleasure in the getting of knowledge. The merchandise of it is better than the merchandise of silver and the gain thereof than fine gold. As we gradually break up fresh ground, decipher that which is obscure, sift out analogies, solve difficulties, and follow out the tracks of history in one continuous line, our enjoyment of study rises to enthusiasm.

In man. Do you not think that the angels perceived the manifold wisdom of God now that they began to understand what man was and what man is? They must have already seen that God had created an order of pure spirits who served Him faithfully and never sinned. There was one form of wisdom displayed in that. Other spirits equally pure went astray, and in the wisdom of God—for there is wisdom in it—these were suffered to continue astray, reserved in chains until the judgment. After awhile the angels perceived that God was about to make another intelligent creature, not altogether spiritual, but a spiritual creature that would be linked with materialism, a creature that would abide in a body of clay. They also perceived that God intended to make this creature a mixture of earth and heaven—such a one that would occupy the place that fallen angels had left vacant. They discerned in this at once the wisdom of God. He had formed a pure spirit; He had fashioned material substances; now He was about to make a creature in which the two should be combined—a creature that should be spiritual and yet would be material.

But, before this creature should be permitted to take his place forever at the right hand of God, he was to be permitted to pass the test of temptation. Being tempted, he was to fall into sin, but out of the condemnation into which he should sink he was to be elevated by an act of grace. Then from the guilt of that sin he was to be cleansed by a matchless system of substitutionary sacrifice. After having been alienated in heart, he should nevertheless become as pure as if he had never been conscious of evil. And contaminated with it he should be redeemed from it and stand in allegiance to the Most High, to serve Him with as absolute a perfection as if he had never transgressed or lost his first estate.

Herein is manifold wisdom, that the Lord God should make so strange a creature that he should be formed of the dust of the ground and yet created in the image of God. A creature that should know sin and whatever of pleasure there might be in it and yet be restored to purity and holiness. A creature who though awhile estranged in heart and guilty of rebelling with a high hand against its Creator should return to its allegiance through the infinitely wise workings of God's Spirit. Henceforth this creature should remain forever the liege servant of God, and something more, the child of God, lifted up and exalted into a nearness of connection and intimacy of communion with the Great Father of Spirits, into which no creature had ever been brought before. In that grand design, the angels must have seen much of the sublime wisdom of God, and that conspicuously through the church.

But, beloved, may not the admiration of angels at the unfolding of this wisdom have been increased by the mystery in which it had long been shrouded from their apprehension? Observe, that Paul was exulting in a revelation "which in other ages was not made known unto the sons of men, as it is now revealed unto his holy apostles and prophets by the Spirit" (Eph. 3:5). What use will he make of it? First he looks around among the saints and sounds the note of welcome. Then he looks out among his fellowman and proclaims it to the Gentile world. At length he looks up and descries among the angelic throng creatures of noble mind and exalted rank, who could sympathize the joy and hail the solution of so grand a problem. Be it remembered that the decree had previously been proclaimed from the throne of the Most High, for "when he bringeth in the firstbegotten into the world, he saith, And let all the angels of God worship him" (Heb. 1:6). Yet the means by which the counsels of God concerning Christ and the church should be brought to pass had not thus far been shown. With what pleasing wonderment, therefore, would the principalities and powers in heavenly places regard the plan as it was unsealed! How well might the apostle look forward to those ages to come that have yet to prove the reality of all that has been foreshadowed, the truth of all that has been prophesied, and (the work now in progress being completed) the actual form and fashion of all that from the beginning was predestinated.

In the union of God and man. Even while the mystery was unexplained, it was not for pure angelic minds to doubt. Still their thoughts must have been full of marvel, and startling questions must have occurred to them. Shall the only-begotten Son of the Father take the nature of man into union with the Godhead? Can it be safe to put such a creature as man into so sublime a relationship with the Creator? Will pride never inflame his breast and provoke his soul to transgress? By what strange process shall he be made meet to partake of the inheritance of the saints in light? While the details are concealed, the destiny seems incomprehensible. It is therefore that the church becomes as a museum that angels may visit with ever-expanding interest and ever-increasing delight. Over the minutest particulars of the divine workmanship in the saints they may pore with pleasure, for there they have open to their observation by the church the manifold wisdom of God. And all this redounds to the glory of the Savior.

That creature, man, when thus elevated can never be proud, for he remembers what he was. If ever the feeling of exultation crosses his mind, he transfers the honor to Christ, who can receive it as His rightful due. There is not in heaven, of all the creatures, a humbler creature, though none more elevated. Made to have dominion over all the works of God's hands with all things put under his feet and made to be akin to Deity itself by virtue of union with the Son of God, man is yet safe to stand there without cause to fear that he should pervert his high prerogative or usurp any adoration or prerogative that does not belong to him. The process through which he has passed—his annealing, as it were, in the fire of his fall and of his repentance, his deep obligations to sovereign grace—shall make it safe to grant that he shall sit with Christ on His throne, even as Christ also overcame and is set down with His Father on His throne. I talk of these things feebly and superficially, but I am persuaded that this is a subject that angels can think of with enchantment, and as they think it over they see transparent proofs of the manifold wisdom of God.

In God bringing honor out of dishonor. But to come down to more familiar topics, probably you will be more impressed with the excellence of this wisdom as you look at the first principles of Christianity than would arrest your attention in any refinements of reasoning. The wisdom of God is clearly seen by angels in this, that though God was dishonored in this world by sin, that sin has redounded to His greater honor. Satan, when he led men astray and tempted them to rebel, thought he had marred the glory of God, but he never did more palpably outwit himself. As Augustine ventured to say of the Fall, "Happy thought." So, when we see how God's mercy and His love have shone resplendent through that dreadful breach, we can only admire the wisdom of God that has thus outmatched the subtlety of hell. The Serpent was exceedingly wise, but God was wiser far. Satan's craft was dexterous, but God's wisdom was infinite in its prescience. Wisdom has outmatched craft. Is it not glorious to think that this world where God was dishonored most is the world where He shall be most revered? There is no such display of the attributes and perfections of Godhead in the whole universe beside as there is here. On our blighted soil God has stood foot to foot with moral evil. God incarnate, the Son of God, has sustained the conflict and won the victory, for while the heel of Christ was bruised, the head of the Dragon has been most effectually broken! A triumph that God would have us commemorate in time and in eternity has come through the sin that threatened the destruction of the world.

In the way redemption was wrought. This wisdom of God is to be seen in the way that our redemption was wrought. The doctrine of substitution is a marvel that, if God had never revealed, none of us could by any possibility have discovered. You remember how it was. We had sinned and were condemned. How could God be gracious and yet be just? How could He keep His law and yet at the same time show His mercy toward us? Of old that problem was solved by the suretyship of Christ. He who had determined to be man put Himself from before the foundation of the world into man's place and offered Himself to God as the head of the race in covenant that He might make recompense to the broken law. Angels could not have conjectured this. But when it was made known to them, how could they refrain to chant fresh songs to the praise of Him who could undertake so loving a responsibility?

It became necessary when Christ was our surety that He should afterward take upon Himself our nature. Oh, how it must have surprised the angels when they heard that the Son of God was coming down to earth to be born of a virgin! What marvel must there have been when the announcement was made through the courts of paradise that He was going down to Bethlehem! One of the angelic number who had been sent to attend Him proclaimed His advent. But while he was making the announcement, "suddenly there was with the angel a multitude of the heavenly host," who now came in to swell the song, "Glory to God in the highest, and on earth peace, good will toward men" (Luke 2:13–14). The swell of that music, how grand! The cadence of those simple words, how charming! Yes, the angels must have discovered something of the wisdom of God when they saw that God thus tabernacled among men—that the Word was made flesh in order to be capable of carrying out His surety engagements and really become a substitute for those who had offended. I think His whole life must have struck them with wonder. They must often have observed wisdom in His actions and in His prayers, in His speech and in His silence. But, when at last He came to die, I think even cherubim and seraphim were wrapped in amazement. That He should stoop from heaven and become a friend to the fallen race might surprise them much, but that He should stoop to die must have appeared utterly incomprehensible. Something more of the love and wisdom of God should yet be revealed to them. I think our hymn must fitly describes how they gathered around that cross:

> And could their eyes have known a tear,
> They must have wept it there.

When they beheld the griefs and torments of the dying Son of God, the Lamb of God's Passover, and when they heard Him say, "It is finished!" (John 19:30), what a door must have been opened to them! They saw then that He had finished transgression, made an end of sin, and brought in an everlasting righteousness. Then, perhaps, they saw more clearly than before how Christ by suffering put an end to our sufferings and by being made a curse for us had made us the righteousness of God in Him. If they marveled during the three days of His slumber in the tomb, His resurrection must have opened up another door to them.

And—when after His forty days' sojourn they came to meet Him with glad acclaim, when they joined Him and with Him rode up to the gates of heaven singing, "Lift up your heads, O ye gates; and be ye lift up, ye everlasting doors; and the King of glory shall come in"; when they came in triumph with "the LORD mighty in battle. . . . the King of glory" (Ps. 24:7–9)—in that procession to His throne, they must still have been more and more amazed and have said one to another, "What thing is this; what mighty marvel! He that became man to suffer is the very one that now rises to reign. He who was born to die now lives forevermore. Behold, He is now the head over all things and made to have dominion over all the works of God's hands, for it has pleased the Father that in Him should all fullness dwell!" Thus, beloved, though time and voice fail me, permit me to say that the whole history of our blessed Lord, who is the Head of the church, is making known to the principalities and powers in heavenly places the manifold wisdom of God in such a way as they never could have otherwise seen it.

In the Holy Spirit's work. The wisdom of God is seen through the church in the Holy Spirit's work as well as in the work of Christ. It is "manifold wisdom." You know the children's toy, the kaleidoscope. Every time you turn it there is some fresh form of beauty. You seldom see the same form twice. So it is with nature, each time and season has its special beauty. There is always variety in its scenery; diversities of form and color are strewn throughout the world. You never saw two hills molded to the same pattern or two rivers that wound after the same fashion from their source down to the sea. Nature is full of variety. So is the work of the Holy Spirit.

In calling sinners to Christ there is singleness of purpose but no uniformity of means. Your conversion, my dear friend, in the main outline is very much like mine, yet your conversion has its distinctive incidents. God's wisdom is displayed equally in bringing you in that way and in bringing me in another way. I believe there will be found evidence at the last of the wisdom of God in the very date, the very place, the very means in and by which every soul is brought to believe in Jesus. Angels will, no doubt, be able to perceive in every conversion some singular marks of beautiful originality proceeding from the inexhaustible Artist of Grace, the Holy Spirit.

In the lives, deaths, and sufferings of the saints. That same wisdom will be seen in the biography of every convert—how the Lord afflicts or how He comforts; how He upholds us, how He keeps back that which cannot yet be endured, how He gently leads us, how He makes us to lie down. We find fault sometimes with the way of providence because we do not understand it. When we shall get a clearer sight of it we shall see that every mark and line was dictated by His love and ordered by His infinite counsel.

As each Christian shall be conformed to the likeness of Christ, angels will see in the products of grace fresh displays of the manifold wisdom of God. I could suppose that the death of a martyr must be such a spectacle as those holy watchers regard with extraordinary interest. Would they not have gathered around such a woman as Blandina, for instance, who was made to sit in a red-hot chair, after having been tossed upon the horns of a wild bull, yet constant to the last she maintained her faith in Christ while passing through the torture? Pure spirits as they were, they must have commiserated the physical anguish and admired the spiritual triumph of this feeble woman thus devoted in her love to their Lord and Master. Yes, you ministering spirits, you who live to serve our Eternal King, surely you must rejoice at the loyalty of those servants of His who die for His truth.

In late years, since this house of prayer was built, when the martyrs of Madagascar were burned at their stakes for Christ, as they stood erect in the fire and began to sing, the angels, celestial vocalists as they are, must have been ravished with a music that they could not emulate. When they breathed the prayer, "Into Thy hands we commend our spirits," the angels must almost have envied them the ability of serving God in that sphere of suffering and the possibility of bearing in their bodies the marks of the Lord Jesus. Aye, and when they have seen your boldness, your constancy, your self-denial, your patience and heard your importunate prayers and groans as you have pleaded for the souls of others, seeking with tears to bring others to Jesus, I do not doubt that they have ascribed to the manifold wisdom of God the production of such luscious fruits from such inferior creatures—fruits that bring to His name so much of glory and so much of renown to His grace. In all the saints, through the history of their vocation and the development of their sanctification, angels can discern the manifold wisdom of God.

The subject is far too large for me. I shall leave you to think it out after thus introducing you to but a few aspects of it. There is much room for meditation as to how these bright and happy spirits do and shall see the wisdom of God in the salvation of the church.

Do Angels Gain Anything by the Church of God?

Do angels gain anything by the church of God? I think they do. Certainly they *acquire increased knowledge*. With us knowledge is sometimes sorrow. To know is often to mourn. What the eye does not see the heart does not rue. "Where ignorance is bliss"—and it sometimes is—there are those who think "'tis folly to be wise." But ignorance is not bliss in heaven. Knowledge increases the joy of the angels, and I will tell you why, because it makes them take a greater delight in God when they see how wise and gracious He is. If it is possible for the angels to be happier than natural innocence and honorable service can render them, they must be happier through knowing and seeing more of God as His attributes are reflected and His perfections mirrored forth in the church.

Angels, I think, *will be enriched by the society of the saints in heaven*. Commerce always enriches, and commerce between angelic and human natures will be enriching to them both. They love in heaven. They show their love by rejoicing over repenting men. They will be glad to see us there. I do believe they will make much of us, as we do if we have seen some poor child reclaimed and afterward grow up to honor. We like to think of such a one. It brings the tears into our eyes that our father did so good a deed for the orphan, the pauper, or the outcast. And will not the angels rejoice over those in whom the Father's mercy has wrought such wonderful happiness?

Again, to my imagining (can it be illusive?) angels are gainers by the church because they *get nearer to the throne of God than they were before*. Another order of beings, our own to wit, is advanced. Surely when one creature gets near to God, all unfallen creatures are promoted. God in vital union with the creature was not to be conceived of until Christ came down to earth and clothed Himself in manhood, thus raising creatureship nearer to God by just that length. So angels by inference seem to me interested in the honor that Jehovah has put on His works—the endowed works of His own formation.

Do you not think, too, that perhaps they *can see God*

better in Christ than even they did before? Is it not possible that even they who formerly did veil their faces with their wings in the presence of the Almighty, because the brightness of glory was excessive, may now stand with unveiled faces and worship God in Christ? I think it is so. They never saw much of God before until they saw God veiled in human flesh. There was too dazzling a splendor for them until the interposing medium of the manhood of Christ came in between them and the absolute Deity. It may be so.

And may not there be a reflex sense of gratitude in the very hearts of angels when they see us in heaven—or while they see us wending our way there—as they perceive what it would have cost to have restored them had they been beguiled by sin and, therefore, what debtors they are to God that they were never suffered to fall? Does it not make their state and standing more and more joyful to them when they see in us how the righteous scarcely are saved, and at what an expense men were lifted up from the ruins of death and the dread doom of the damned? Why, I think they say not one to another with pharisaism: "We thank You, great God, that we are not as men are." No, they say with lowliness of mind: "We bless You, O God, that we were permitted to stand in our fidelity and were not left to the natural weakness that might have succumbed to temptation. For You charged even Your angels with folly, but You have held us and here we are to bless Your name." It may be so; it may be so.

What Is All This to Us?

What is all this to us? *Ought it not to make us prize the Gospel?* If the angels think so much of it, oh! what should we think? If they who have only seen it esteem it so, how ought we to value it who have tasted it? If they admire the veins that filled the fountain, what shall we say who have washed in that fountain? If they wonder at Christ, who took not on Him the nature of angels, how shall we admire Him who espoused the house of Abraham and the seed of Adam? Let us appreciate the Gospel beyond all price, emolument, or honor.

How, too, *should we study it,* if it be the research of angelic intellects! Is the church their schoolbook whence they learn lessons of the divine wisdom because no science is equal to that of the wisdom of God in Christ revealed in His church? O be not, converts, ignorant of the Word of God. Do not be oblivious of the operations of God in your own souls! The angels desire to look into these things. Do you look into them? Blessed shall you be if you abide in the study of the Word of God! You shall be like trees planted by the rivers of water that bring forth their fruit in their season. O do apply every faculty you have to acquire increasing knowledge of that which angels love to study.

And now take courage, you feebleminded ones, and *never fear again the sneer of the man who calls the Gospel folly.* Account him to be the victim of folly who despises this manifold wisdom. Shall I set the judgment of a poor, puny mortal against the judgment of an angel? I suppose that even Newton, Kepler, Locke, and those mighty master spirits would be mere infants compared with seraphs. Those great men loved to study the Scriptures. When your modern pretenders to a little smack of philosophy come in and sneer at our holy Gospel, we can well afford to sneer at them. What are their sneers to us? In proportion to a man's ignorance is generally his impudence when he meddles with the Gospel. I think it was Hume who confessed that he had never read the New Testament and said he never would. Yet he was one of the most glib in caviling at that of which he knew nothing. Ah! you skeptics, sciolists, and scoffers, we can well afford to let you rail. But you can ill afford to rail when angels are awed into wonder, and so would you be if there were anything angelic about your temper or anything of right wisdom in your attainments.

Last of all, if this be so, *how we who have a saving interest in it ought to love Christ, and how they ought to tremble who have it not!* Unsaved men, unsaved women, if it wants manifold wisdom to save man, then man's ruin must be very great, and your peril must be very imminent. If it amazes angels to see how God saves, it must be a terrible destruction from which He saves. That destruction is coming upon you. Its dark shadows have already begun to gather around you. How great your folly to refuse a salvation so wise, to reject a Savior so attractive as Jesus! Consider His loving gentleness and the simple way in which He saves—believe and live. The supplies necessary for your salvation are all waiting. There is nothing to be done; it is all complete. There is nothing to be found; it is all ready. Salvation is finished. What a fool must he be that will not have it! O stretch out your withered hand and take it! God give you power. If you say, "How?" I answer thus: Trust, trust, trust. Come and confide in Christ. Rely upon Christ and He will save you. God grant you grace to do it at once, and He shall have the praise. Amen.

NOTES

Of Good Angels

John Wesley (1703–1781), with his brother Charles and with George Whitefield, founded the Methodist movement in Britain and America. On May 24, 1738, he had his great spiritual experience in a meeting at Aldersgate Street, when his "heart was strangely warmed" and he received assurance of salvation. Encouraged by Whitefield to do open-air preaching, Wesley soon was addressing thousands in spite of the fact that many churches were closed to him. The Methodist societies he formed became local churches that conserved the results of his evangelism. He wrote many books and preached 40,000 sermons during his long ministry.

This sermon was taken from *The Works of John Wesley,* volume 6, published by Zondervan Publishing House.

John Wesley

11

OF GOOD ANGELS

Are they not all ministering spirits, sent forth to minister for them who shall be heirs of salvation? (Hebrews 1:14).

MANY OF THE ancient heathens had (probably from tradition) some notion of good and evil angels. They had some conception of a superior order of beings between men and God, whom the Greeks generally termed demons *(knowing ones),* and the Romans, genii. Some of these they supposed to be kind and benevolent, delighting in doing good; others, to be malicious and cruel, delighting in doing evil. But their conceptions both of one and the other were crude, imperfect, and confused, being only fragments of truth partly delivered down by their forefathers and partly borrowed from the inspired writings.

Of the former, the benevolent kind seems to have been the celebrated demon of Socrates, concerning which so many and so various conjectures have been made in succeeding ages. "This gives me notice," said he, "every morning, of any evil which will befall me that day." A late writer, indeed (I suppose one that hardly believes the existence of either angel or spirit), has published a dissertation wherein he labors to prove that the demon of Socrates was only his reason. But it was not the manner of Socrates to speak in such obscure and ambiguous terms. If he had meant his reason, he would doubtless have said so. But this could not be his meaning. For it was impossible his reason should give him notice every morning of every evil that would befall him in that day. It does not lie within the province of reason to give such notice of future contingencies. Neither does this odd interpretation in anyway agree with the inference which he himself draws from it. "My demon," says he, "did not give me notice this morning of any evil that was to befall

125

me today. Therefore I cannot regard as any evil my being condemned to die." Undoubtedly it was some spiritual being, probably one of these ministering spirits.

An ancient poet, one who lived several ages before Socrates, speaks more determinately on this subject. Hesiod does not scruple to say, "Millions of spiritual creatures walk the earth unseen." Hence, it is probable, arose the numerous tales about the exploits of their demigods: *Minorum gentium.* Hence their satyrs, fauns, and nymphs of every kind wherewith they supposed both the sea and land to be filled. But how empty, childish, and unsatisfactory are all the accounts they give of them as, indeed, accounts that depend upon broken, uncertain tradition can hardly fail to be.

Revelation only is able to supply this defect. This only gives us a clear, rational, consistent account of those whom our eyes have not seen nor our ears heard—of both good and evil angels. It is my design to speak, at present, only of the former, of whom we have a full, though brief account in these words: "Are they not all ministering spirits, sent forth to minister for them who shall be heirs of salvation?"

What Are Ministering Angels?

The question in this text is, according to the manner of the apostle, equivalent to a strong affirmation. And hence we learn, first, that with regard to their essence or nature, they are all spirits. They are not material beings clogged with flesh and blood like us. But having bodies, if any, they are not gross and earthly like ours, but are of a finer substance resembling fire or flame more than any other of these lower elements. And is not something like this intimated in those words of the psalmist: "Who maketh his angels spirits, and his ministers a flame of fire?" (Ps. 104:4). As spirits, God has endued them with understanding, will or affections (which are indeed the same thing, as the affections are only the will exerting itself various ways), and liberty. And are not these—understanding, will, and liberty—essential to, if not the essence of, a spirit?

But who of the children of men can comprehend what is the understanding of an angel? Who can comprehend how far their sight extends? Analogous to sight in men, though not the same (but thus we are constrained to speak through the poverty of human language), probably not only over one hemisphere of the earth, yea, or, "Ten-fold the length of this terrene" or even of the solar system, but so far as to take in one view the whole extent of the creation! And we cannot conceive any defect in their perception neither any error in their understanding. But in what manner do they use their understanding? We must in nowise imagine that they creep from one truth to another by that slow method which we call reasoning. Undoubtedly they see, at one glance, whatever truth is presented to their understanding, and that with all the certainty and clearness that we mortals see the most self-evident axiom.

Who then can conceive the extent of their knowledge, not only of the nature, attributes, and works of God, whether of creation or providence, but of the circumstances, actions, words, tempers, and even thoughts of men? For although God only "knowest the hearts of all men" (Acts 1:24) and "known unto God are all his works," together with the changes they undergo, "from the beginning of the world" (15:18), yet we cannot doubt but His angels know the hearts of those to whom they more immediately minister. Much less can we doubt of their knowing the thoughts that are in our hearts at any particular time. What should hinder their seeing them as they arise? Not the thin veil of flesh and blood. Can these intercept the view of a spirit? No!

> Walls within walls no more its passage bar,
> Than unopposing space of liquid air.

Far more easily, then, and far more perfectly, than we can read a man's thoughts in his face do these sagacious beings read our thoughts just as they rise in our hearts, inasmuch as they see the kindred spirit more clearly than we see the body. If this seems strange to any who had not adverted to it before, let him only consider: Suppose my spirit was out of the body, could not an angel see my thoughts even without my uttering any words (if words are used in the world of spirits)? And cannot that ministering spirit see them just as well now while I am in the body? It seems, therefore, to be an unquestionable truth (although perhaps not commonly observed) that angels know not only the words and actions, but also the thoughts, of those to whom they minister. And, indeed, without this knowledge they would be very ill qualified to perform various parts of their ministry.

And what an inconceivable degree of wisdom must they have acquired by the use of their amazing faculties, over and above that with which they were originally endued, in the course of more than six thousand years! (That they have existed so long we are assured, for they "sang together when the foundations of the earth were laid.") How immensely must their wisdom have increased during so long a period, not only by surveying the hearts and ways of men in their successive generations, but by observing the works of God—His works of creation, His works of providence, His works of grace—and, above all, "in heaven their angels do always behold the face of my Father which is in heaven" (Matt. 18:10).

What measures of holiness, as well as wisdom, have they derived from this inexhaustible ocean!

> A boundless, fathomless abyss,
> Without a bottom or a shore!

Are they not hence by way of eminence styled *the holy angels?* What goodness, what philanthropy, what love to man have they drawn from those rivers that are at His right hand! Such as we cannot conceive to be exceeded by any but that of God our Savior. And they are still drinking in more love from this fountain of living water.

Such is the knowledge and wisdom of the angels of God as we learn from His own oracles. Such are their holiness and goodness. And how astonishing is their strength! Even a fallen angel is styled by an inspired writer, "the prince of the power of the air" (Eph. 2:2). How terrible a proof did he give of this power in suddenly raising the whirlwind which "smote the four corners of the house"

(Job 1:19) and destroyed all the children of Job at once! That this was his work we may easily learn from the command to save Job's life (2:6). But he gave a far more terrible proof of his strength (if we suppose that "messenger of the Lord" to have been an evil angel, as is not at all improbable) when he smote with death 185,000 men in one night—no, possibly in one hour, if not one moment (see 2 Kings 19:35). Yet a strength abundantly greater than this must have been exerted by that angel (whether he was an angel of light or of darkness, which is not determined by the text) who smote, in one hour, all "the firstborn of Egypt, both of man and beast" (Ps. 135:8). For considering the extent of the land of Egypt, the immense populousness thereof, and the innumerable cattle fed in their houses and grazing in their fruitful fields, the men and beasts who were slain in that night must have amounted to several millions!

And if this be supposed to have been an evil angel, must not a good angel be as strong, yea, stronger than him? For surely any good angel must have more power than even an archangel ruined. And what power must the "four angels" in the book of Revelation have who were appointed to "hold the four winds of earth" (7:1)! There seems, therefore, no extravagance in supposing that, if God were pleased to permit, any of the angels of light could heave the earth and all the planets out of their orbits. Yes, He could arm Himself with all these elements and crush the whole frame of nature. Indeed we do not know how to set any bounds to the strength of these first-born children of God.

And although none but their great Creator is omni-present—although none beside Him can ask, "Do not I fill heaven and earth?" (Jer. 23:24)—yet, undoubtedly, He has given an immense sphere of action (though not unbounded) to created spirits. "The prince of the king-dom of Persia" (Dan. 10:13), though probably an evil angel, seems to have had a sphere of action, both of knowledge and power, as extensive as that vast empire. The same, if not greater, we may reasonably ascribe to the good angel whom he withstood for twenty-one days.

The angels of God have great power, in particular, over the human body—power either to cause or remove pain and diseases, either to kill or to heal. They perfectly well understand whereof we are made. They know all the springs of this curious machine and can, doubtless, by God's permission, touch any of them so as either to stop or restore its motion. Of this power, even in an evil angel, we have a clear instance in the case of Job, whom he "smote with sore boils from the sole of his foot unto his crown" (2:7). And in that instant, undoubtedly, he would have killed him if God had not saved his life. And, on the other hand, of the power of angels to heal, we have a remarkable instance in the case of Daniel. "There remained no strength in me," said the prophet, "neither was there breath left in me. Then there came again and touched me one like the appearance of a man, and he strengthened me. And said, O man greatly beloved, fear not: peace be unto thee, be strong, yea, be strong. And when he had spoken unto me, I was strengthened" (Dan. 10:17–19).

On the other hand, when they are commissioned from above, may they not put a period to human life? There is nothing improbable in what Dr. Parnell supposes the angel to say to the hermit concerning the death of the child:

> To all but thee, in fits he seem'd to go:
> And 'twas my ministry to deal the blow.

From this great truth, the heathen poets probably derived their imagination that Iris used to be sent down from heaven to discharge souls out of their bodies. And perhaps the sudden death of many of the children of God may be owing to the ministry of an angel.

So perfectly are the angels of God qualified for their high office, it remains to inquire how they discharge their office.

How Do Angels Minister to the Heirs of Salvation?

I will not say that they do not minister at all to those who, through their obstinate impenitence and unbelief, disinherit themselves of the kingdom. This world is a world of mercy, wherein God pours down many mercies, even on the evil and the unthankful. And many of these, it is probable, are conveyed even to them by the ministry of angels, especially so long as they have any thought of God or any fear of God before their eyes. But it is their favorite employ, their peculiar office, to minister to the heirs of salvation—to those who are now saved by faith or at least seeking God in sincerity.

Is it not their first care to minister to our souls? But we must not expect this will be done with observation, in such a manner as that we may clearly distinguish their working from the workings of our own minds. We have no more reason to look for this than for their appearing in a visible shape. Without this they can, in a thousand ways, apply to our understanding. They may assist us in our search after truth, remove many doubts and difficulties, throw light on what was before dark and obscure, and confirm us in the truth that is after godliness. They may warn us of evil in disguise and place what is good in a clear, strong light. They may gently move our wills to embrace what is good and to fly from that which is evil. They may, many times, quicken our dull affections, increase our holy hopes or filial fears, and assist us more ardently to love Him who has first loved us. Yea, they may be sent of God to answer that whole prayer put into our mouths by pious Bishop Ken:

> O may thy angels, while I sleep,
> Around my bed their vigils keep;
> Their love angelical instil,
> Stop every avenue of ill!
> May they celestial joys rehearse,
> And thought to thought with me converse!

Although the manner of this we shall not be able to explain while we dwell in the body.

May they not minister also to us, with respect to our bodies, in a thousand ways that we do not now understand? They may prevent our falling into many dangers, which we are not sensible of, and they may deliver us out of many others, though we know not from where our deliverance comes. How many times have we been strangely and unaccountably preserved in sudden and dangerous falls! And it is well if we did not impute that preservation to chance or to our own wisdom or strength. Not so! It was God gave His angels charge over us, and in their hands they bore us up. Indeed, men of the world will always impute such deliverances to accident or second causes. To these, possibly, some of them might have imputed Daniel's preservation in the lions' den. But Daniel himself ascribes it to the true cause: "My God hath sent his angel, and shut the lions' mouths" (Dan. 6:22).

When a violent disease, supposed incurable, is totally and suddenly removed, it is by no means improbable that this is effected by the ministry of an angel. And perhaps it is owing to the same cause that a remedy is unaccountably suggested either to the sick person or some attending upon him by which he is entirely cured.

It seems what are usually called divine dreams may be frequently ascribed to angels. We have a remarkable instance of this kind related by one who would hardly be thought an enthusiast, for he was a heathen, a philosopher, and an emperor. I mean Marcus Antoninus. In his meditations, he solemnly thanks God for revealing to him, when he was at Cajeta, in a dream, what totally cured the bloody flux, which none of his physicians were able to heal. And why may we not suppose that God gave him this notice by the ministry of an angel?

And how often does God deliver us from evil men by the ministry of his angels! Overturning whatever their rage or malice or subtlety had plotted against us. These are about their bed, about their path, and privy to all their dark designs. Many of them, undoubtedly, they brought to nothing by means that we think not of. Sometimes they blast their favorite schemes in the beginning and sometimes when they are just ripe for execution. And this they can do by a thousand means that we are not aware of. They can check them in their midcareer by bereaving them of courage or strength, by striking faintness through their loins, or by turning their wisdom into foolishness. Sometimes they bring to light the hidden things of darkness and show us the traps that are laid for our feet. In these and various other ways, they hew the snares of the ungodly in pieces.

Another grand branch of their ministry is to counter work of evil angels who are continually going about not only as roaring lions seeking whom they may devour but, more dangerously still, as angels of light seeking whom they may deceive. And how great is the number of these! Are they not as the stars of heaven for multitude? How great is their subtlety matured by the experience of above six thousand years. How great is their strength! It is only inferior to that of the angels of God. The strongest of the sons of men are but as grasshoppers before them. And what an advantage have they over us by that single circumstance, that they are invisible! As we have not strength to repel their force, so we have not skill to decline it. But the merciful Lord has not given us up to the will of our enemies: "The eyes of the LORD," that is, His holy angels, "run to and fro throughout the whole earth" (2 Chron. 16:9). And if our eyes were opened we would see that they are more that are for us than they that are against us (see 2 Kings 6:16). We should see,

> A convoy attends,
> A ministering host of invisible friends.

And whenever those assault us in soul or in body, these are able, willing, and ready to defend us, who are at least equally strong, equally wise, and equally vigilant. And who can hurt us while we have armies of angels, the God of angels, on our side?

And we may make one general observation: Whatever assistance God gives to men by men, the same, and frequently in a higher degree, He gives to them by angels. Does He administer to us by men light when we are in darkness, joy when we are in heaviness, deliverance when we are in danger, ease and health when we are sick or in pain? It cannot be doubted, but He frequently conveys the same blessings by the ministry of angels. It is not so sensibly, indeed, but full as effectually though the messengers are not seen. Does He frequently deliver us by means of men from the violence and subtlety of our enemies? Many times He works the same deliverance by those invisible agents. These shut the mouths of the human lions so that they have no power to hurt us. And frequently they join with our human friends (although neither they nor we are sensible of it), giving them wisdom, courage, or strength, without which all their labor for us would be unsuccessful. Thus do they secretly minister, in numberless instances, to the heirs of salvation, while we hear only the voices of men and see none but men around us.

But does not the Scripture teach the help which is done upon earth, God doeth it Himself? (see Ps. 121:2). Most certainly He does. And He is able to do it by His own immediate power. He has no need of using any instruments at all, either in heaven or earth. He needs not either angels or men to fulfill the whole counsel of His will. But it is not His pleasure so to work. He never did, and we may reasonably suppose He never will. He has always wrought by such instruments as He pleases. But still it is God Himself that does the work. Whatever help, therefore, we have either by angels or men is as much the work of God as if He were to put forth His almighty arm and work without any means at all. But He has used them from the beginning of the world. In all ages He has used the ministry both of men and angels. And hereby, especially, is seen "by the church the manifold wisdom of God" (Eph. 3:10). Meantime the same glory redounds to Him as if He used no instruments at all.

The grand reason why God is pleased to assist men by men, rather than immediately by Himself, is undoubtedly to endear us to each other by these mutual good offices in order to increase our happiness both in time and eternity. And is it not for the same reason that God is pleased to give His angels charge over us? Namely, that He may endear us and them to each other and that by the increase of our love and gratitude to them, we may find a proportionable increase of happiness when we meet in our Father's kingdom. In the meantime, though we may not worship them (worship is due only to our common Creator), yet we may "esteem them very highly in love for their work's sake" (1 Thess. 5:13). And we may imitate them in all holiness, suiting our lives to the prayer our Lord Himself has taught us and laboring to do His will on earth as angels do it in heaven.

I cannot conclude this discourse better than in that admirable collect of our church:

> O everlasting God, who hast ordained and constituted the services of angels and men in a wonderful manner; grant that as thy holy angels alway do thee service in heaven, so by thy appointment they may succour and defend us on earth, through Jesus Christ our Lord.

Of Evil Angels

John Wesley (1703–1781), with his brother Charles and with George Whitefield, founded the Methodist movement in Britain and America. On May 24, 1738, he had his great spiritual experience in a meeting at Aldersgate Street, when his "heart was strangely warmed" and he received assurance of salvation. Encouraged by Whitefield to do open-air preaching, Wesley soon was addressing thousands in spite of the fact that many churches were closed to him. The Methodist societies he formed became local churches that conserved the results of his evangelism. He wrote many books and preached 40,000 sermons during his long ministry.

This sermon was taken from *The Works of John Wesley,* volume 6, published by Zondervan Publishing House.

John Wesley

12

OF EVIL ANGELS

For we wrestle not against flesh and blood, but against principalities, against powers, against the rulers of the darkness of this world, against spiritual wickedness in high places (Ephesians 6:12).

IT HAS BEEN frequently observed that there are no gaps or chasms in the creation of God but that all the parts of it are admirably connected together to make up one universal whole. Accordingly, there is one chain of beings from the lowest to the highest point, from an unorganized particle of earth or water to Michael the archangel. And the scale of creatures does not advance *per saltum,* by leaps, but by smooth and gentle degrees, although it is true these are frequently imperceptible to our imperfect faculties. We cannot accurately trace many of the intermediate links of this amazing chain, which are abundantly too fine to be discerned either by our senses or understanding.

We can only observe in a gross and general manner, rising one above another, first, inorganical earth; then, minerals and vegetables, in their several orders; afterward, insects, reptiles, fishes, beasts, men, and angels. Of angels, indeed, we know nothing with any certainty but by revelation. The accounts that are left by the wisest of the ancients or given by the modern heathens being no better than silly, self-inconsistent fables, too gross to be imposed even upon children. But by divine revelation we are informed that they were all created holy and happy, yet they did not all continue as they were created. Some kept, but some left, their first estate. The former of these are now good angels; the latter, evil angels. Of the former, I have spoken in the preceding discourse. I purpose now to speak of the latter. And highly necessary it is that we should well understand what God has revealed concerning them that they may gain no advantage over us by our ignorance and that we may know how to wrestle against them effectually. For we wrestle not against flesh and blood, but against principalities, against powers, against the rulers of the darkness of this world, against wicked spirits in heavenly places.

This single passage seems to contain the whole scriptural doctrine concerning evil angels. I apprehend the plain meaning of it, literally translated, is this: "Our wrestling" (the wrestling of real Christians) "is not" only, or chiefly, "against flesh and blood" (weak men, or fleshly appetites and passions), "but against principalities, against powers" (the mighty princes of all the infernal regions with their combined forces). And great is their power, as is also the power of the legions they command—"against the rulers of the world." (This is the literal meaning of the word.) Perhaps these principalities and powers remain chiefly in the citadel of their kingdom. But there are other evil spirits that range abroad to whom the provinces of the world are committed—"of the darkness" (chiefly the spiritual darkness) "of this world," which prevails during the present state of things, "against wicked spirits"—eminently such. They mortally hate and continually oppose holiness and labor to infuse unbelief, pride, evil desire, malice, anger, hatred, envy, or revenge "in heavenly places," which were once their abode and which they still aspire after.

In prosecuting this important subject, I will endeavor to explain the nature and properties of evil angels and their employment.

The Nature and Properties of Evil Angels

With regard to the nature and properties of evil angels, we cannot doubt but all the angels of God were originally of the same nature. Unquestionably they were the highest order of created beings. They were spirits—pure ethereal creatures, simple and incorruptible; if not wholly immaterial, yet certainly not encumbered with gross, earthly flesh and blood. As spirits, they were endued with understanding, with affections, and with liberty or a power of self-determination, so that it lay in themselves either to continue in their allegiance to God or to rebel against Him.

And their original properties were, doubtless, the same with those of the holy angels. There is no absurdity in supposing Satan their chief—otherwise styled, "Lucifer, son of the morning" (Isa. 14:12)—to have been at least one of the first, if not the first archangel. Like the other sons of the morning, they had a height and depth of understanding quite incomprehensible to us. In consequence of this they had such knowledge and wisdom that the wisest of the children of men (had men then existed) would have been mere idiots in comparison of them. Their strength was equal to their knowledge, such as it cannot enter into our hearts to conceive. Neither can we conceive to how wide a sphere of action either their strength or their knowledge extended. Their number God alone can tell. Doubtless it was only less than infinite. And a third part of these stars of heaven the archrebel drew after him.

We do not exactly know (because it is not revealed in the oracles of God) either what was the occasion of their apostasy or what effect it immediately produced upon them. Some have, not improbably, supposed that when God published "the decree" (mentioned Ps. 2:6–7) concerning the kingdom of His only-begotten Son to be over all creatures, these firstborn of creatures gave place to pride, comparing themselves to Him. This supposition is possibly intimated by the very name of Satan, Lucifer, or Michael, which means, "Who is like God?" It may be Satan, then first giving way to temptation, said in his heart, I too will have my throne. "I will sit also upon the mount of the congregation, in the sides of the north, . . . I will be like the most High" (Isa. 14:13–14). But how did the mighty then fall! What an amazing loss did they sustain! If we allow of them all what our poet supposes concerning their chief in particular:

> His form had not yet lost
> All its original brightness, nor appear'd

> Less than archangel ruin'd, and the excess
> Of glory obscured—

if we suppose their outward form was not entirely changed (though it must have been in a great degree because the evil disposition of the mind must dim the luster of the visage), yet what an astonishing change was wrought within when angels became devils! when the holiest of all the creatures of God became the most unholy!

From the time that they shook off their allegiance to God, they shook off all goodness and contracted all those tempers that are most hateful to Him and most opposite to His nature. And ever since, they are full of pride, arrogance, haughtiness, exalting themselves above measure. Although so deeply depraved through their inmost frame, yet they are admiring their own perfections. They are full of envy, if not against God Himself (and even that is not impossible, seeing they formerly aspired after His throne), yet against all their fellow creatures—against the angels of God, who now enjoy the heaven from which they fell, and much more against those worms of the earth who are now called to "inherit the kingdom" (Matt. 25:34). They are full of cruelty and of rage against all the children of men, whom they long to inspire with the same wickedness as themselves and to involve in the same misery.

In the prosecution of this infernal design, they are diligent in the highest degree. To find out the most effectual means of putting it into execution, they apply to this end the whole force of their angelical understanding. They second it with their whole strength, so far as God is pleased to permit. But it is well for mankind that God has set them bounds that they cannot pass. He has said to the fiercest and strongest of the apostate spirits, "Hitherto shalt thou come, but no further" (Job 38:11). Otherwise, how easily and how quickly might one of them overturn the whole frame of nature! How soon would they involve all in one common ruin or, at least, destroy man from the face of the earth! And they are indefatigable in their bad work: They never are faint or weary. Indeed, it seems no spirits are capable of weariness but those that inhabit flesh and blood.

One circumstance more we may learn from the Scripture concerning the evil angels: They do not wander at large but are all united under one common head. It is he that is styled by our blessed Lord, "the prince of this world" (John 12:31; 14:30; 16:11). Yes, the apostle Paul does not scruple to call him, "the god of this world" (2 Cor. 4:4). He is frequently styled Satan, the Adversary, being the great adversary both of God and man. He is termed "the Devil," by way of eminence; "Apollyon," or the destroyer; "the old serpent," from his beguiling Eve under that form; and "the angel of the bottomless pit." We have reason to believe that the other evil angels are under his command; that they are ranged by him according to their several orders; that they are appointed to their several stations and have, from time to time, their several works and offices assigned them. And, undoubtedly, they are connected (though we know not how—certainly not by love) both to him and to each other.

The Employment of Evil Angels

Evil angels are (remember, so far as God permits!) χοσμοχρατορες, "governors of the world"! So that there may be more ground than we are apt to imagine for that strange expression of Satan when he showed our Lord "all the kingdoms of the world, and the glory of them; and saith unto him, All these things will I give thee, if thou wilt fall down and worship me" (Matt. 4:8–9). It is a little more particularly expressed in the fourth chapter of Luke: "The devil . . . shewed unto him all the kingdoms of the world in a moment of time." (Such an astonishing measure of power is still left in the Prince of Darkness!) "And the devil said unto him, All this power will I give thee, and the glory of them: for that is delivered unto me; and to whomsoever I will I give it" (vv. 5–6). They are "the rulers of the darkness of this [age]" (so the words are literally translated), of the present state of things, during which "the whole world lieth in wickedness" (1 John 5:19). He is the element of the children of men, only those who fear God being excepted. He and his angels, in connection with and in subordination to him, dispose all the ignorance, all the error, all the folly, and, particularly, all the wickedness of men in such a manner as may most hinder the kingdom of God and most advance the kingdom of darkness.

But has every man a particular evil angel, as well as a good one, attending him? This has been an exceeding ancient opinion, both among the Christians and the Jews before them. But it is much doubted whether it can be sufficiently proved from Scripture. Indeed it would not be improbable that there is a particular evil angel with every man, if we were assured there is a good one. But this cannot be inferred from those words of our Lord concerning little children: "in heaven their angels do always behold the face of my Father which is in heaven" (Matt. 18:10). This only proves that there are angels who are appointed to take care of little children. It does not prove that a particular angel is allotted to every child. Neither is it proved by the words of Rhoda's companions who, when she reported hearing the voice of Peter, said, "It is his angel" (Acts 12:15). We cannot infer any more from this, even suppose "his angel" means his guardian angel, than that they believed the doctrine of guardian angels, which was then common among the Jews. But still it will remain a disputable point (seeing revelation determines nothing concerning it) whether every man is attended either by a particular good or a particular evil angel.

But whether or not any particular men are attended by particular evil spirits, we know that Satan and all his angels are continually warring against us and watching over all the children of men. They are ever watching to see whose outward or inward circumstances, whose prosperity or adversity, whose health or sickness, whose friends or enemies, whose youth or age, whose knowledge or ignorance, whose blindness or idleness, whose joys or sorrows may lay them open to temptation. And they are perpetually ready to make the utmost advantage of every circumstance. These skillful wrestlers espy the smallest slip we make and avail themselves of it immediately, as they also are about our beds, and about our paths, and spy out all our ways. Indeed each of them "as a roaring lion, walketh about, seeking whom he may devour" (1 Peter 5:8) or whom he may beguile through his subtlety "as the serpent beguiled Eve" (2 Cor. 11:3). Yes, and in order to do this the more effectually, they transform themselves into angels of light. Thus,

> With rage that never ends,
> Their hellish arts they try;
> Legions of dire, malicious fiends,
> And spirits enthroned on high.

It is by these instruments chiefly that the "foolish heart" of those who know not God "was darkened" (Rom. 1:21). Yes, they frequently darken, in a measure, the hearts of those that do know God. The "god of this world" knows how to blind our hearts, to spread a cloud over our understanding, and to obscure the light of those truths that, at other times, shine as bright as the noonday sun. By this means he assaults our faith, our evidence of things unseen. He endeavors to weaken that hope full of immortality to which God had begotten us, and thereby to lessen, if he cannot destroy, our joy in God our Savior. But, above all, he strives to dampen our love of God, as he knows this is the spring of all our religion and that, as this rises or falls, the work of God flourishes or decays in the soul.

Next to the love of God, there is nothing that Satan so deeply abhors as the love of neighbor. He uses, therefore, every possible means to prevent or destroy this; to excite either private or public suspicions, animosities, resentment, quarrels; to destroy the peace of families or of nations; and to banish unity and concord from the earth. And this, indeed, is the triumph of his art: to embitter the poor, miserable children of men against each other and, at length, urge them to do his own work to plunge one another into the pit of destruction.

This enemy of all righteousness is equally diligent to hinder every good word and work. If he cannot prevail upon us to do evil, he will, if possible, prevent our doing good. He is peculiarly diligent to hinder the work of God from spreading in the hearts of men. What pains does he take to prevent or obstruct the general work of God! And how many are his devices to stop its progress in particular souls; to hinder their continuing or growing in grace and in the knowledge of our Lord Jesus Christ; to lessen, if not destroy, that love, joy, peace, long-suffering, gentleness, goodness, fidelity, meekness, temperance that our Lord works by His loving Spirit in those that believe and wherein the very essence of religion consists.

To effect these ends, he is continually laboring with all his skill and power to infuse evil thoughts of every kind into the hearts of men. And certainly it is easy for a spirit to speak to our hearts as for a man to speak to our ears. But sometimes it is exceeding difficult to distinguish these from our own thoughts—those which he injects so exactly resembling those which naturally arise in our own minds. Sometimes, indeed, we may distinguish one from the other by this circumstance: The thoughts that naturally arise in our minds are generally, if not always, occasioned by, or at least connected with, some inward or outward circumstance that went before. But those that are preternaturally suggested have frequently no relation to or connection (at least, none that we are able to discern) with anything that preceded. On the contrary, they shoot in, as it were, across and thereby show that they are of a different growth.

He likewise labors to awaken evil passions or tempers in our souls. He endeavors to inspire those passions and tempers that are directly opposite to the fruit of the Spirit. He strives to instill unbelief, atheism, ill-will, bitterness, hatred, malice, envy—opposite to faith and love; fear, sorrow, anxiety, worldly care—opposite to peace and joy; impatience, ill-nature, anger, resentment—opposite to long-suffering, gentleness, meekness; fraud, guile, dissimulation—contrary to fidelity; love of the world, inordinate affection, foolish desires—opposite to the love of God. One sort of evil desires he may probably raise or inflame by touching the springs of this animal machine, endeavoring thus, by means of the body, to disturb or sully the soul.

And, in general, we may observe that as no good is done, spoken, or thought by any man without the assistance of God working together in and with those that believe in Him, so there is no evil done, spoken, or thought without the assistance of the Devil, who worketh with energy, with strong, though secret power, in the children of unbelief. Thus he "entered . . . into Judas" (Luke 22:3), and confirmed him in the design of betraying his Master. Thus he put it in the hearts of Ananias and Sapphira "to lie to the Holy Ghost" (Acts 5:3). And, in like manner, he has a share in all the actions and words and designs of evil men. As the children of God are "workers together with him" (2 Cor. 6:1) in every good thought, word, or action, so the children of the Devil are workers together with him in every evil thought, word, or work. So that as all good tempers, and remotely all good words and actions, are the fruit of the good Spirit, in like manner, all evil tempers, with all the words and works that spring from them, are the fruit of the evil spirit, inasmuch that all the "works of the flesh" (of the evil nature) are likewise the work of the Devil.

On this account, because he is continually inciting men to evil, he is emphatically called "the Tempter." Nor is it only with regard to his own children that he is thus employed, he is continually tempting the children of God also and those that are laboring so to be.

> A constant watch he keeps;
>   He eyes them night and day;
> He never slumbers, never sleeps,
>   Lest he should lose his prey.

Indeed, the holiest of men, as long as they remain upon earth, are not exempt from his temptations. They cannot expect it, seeing "it is enough for the disciple that he be as his master" (Matt. 10:25). And we know He was tempted to evil until He said, "Father, into thy hands I commend my spirit" (Luke 23:46).

For such is the malice of the Wicked One that he will

torment whom he cannot destroy. If he cannot entice men to sin, he will, so far as he is permitted, put them to pain. There is no doubt but he is the occasion, directly or indirectly, of many of the pains of humankind, which those who cannot otherwise account for them lightly pass over as nervous. And innumerable accidents, as they are called, are undoubtedly owing to his agency—such as the unaccountable fright or falling of horses; the overturning of carriages; the breaking or dislocating of bones; the hurt done by the falling or burning of houses; the calamities caused by storms of wind, snow, rain, hail, lightning, or earthquakes. But to all these, and a thousand more, this subtle spirit can give the appearance of accidents, for fear the sufferers, if they knew the real agents, should call on One for help that is stronger than he.

There is little reason to doubt but many diseases likewise, both of the acute and chronic kind, are either occasioned or increased by diabolical agency—particularly those that begin in an instant without any discernible cause, as well as those that continue and, perhaps, gradually increase in spite of all the power of medicine. Here, indeed, "vain [man] would be wise" (Job 11:12), again calling in the nerves to their assistance. But is not this explaining *ignotum per ignotius,* "a thing unknown by what is more unknown"? For what do we know of the nerves themselves? Not even whether they are solid or hollow!

Many years ago I was asking an experienced physician, one particularly eminent for curing lunacy, "Sir, have you not seen reason to believe that some lunatics are really demoniacs?" He answered, "Sir, I have been often inclined to think that most lunatics are demoniacs. Nor is there any weight in that objection that they are frequently cured by medicine, for so might any other disease occasioned by an evil spirit if God did not suffer him to repeat the stroke by which that disease is occasioned."

This thought opens to a wider scene. Who can tell how many of those diseases that we impute altogether to natural causes may be really preternatural? What disorder is there in the human frame that an evil angel may not inflict? Cannot he smite us as he did Job, and that in a moment with boils from the crown of the head to the sole of the foot? Cannot he with equal ease inflict any other either external or internal malady? Could not he in a moment, by divine permission, cast the strongest man down to the ground and make him wallow foaming with all the symptoms either of epilepsy or apoplexy? In like manner, it is easy for him to smite any one man or everyone in a city or nation with a malignant fever or with the plague itself, so that vain would be the help of man.

But that malice blinds the eyes of the wise, one would imagine so intelligent a being would not stoop so low, as it seems the Devil sometimes does, to torment the poor children of men! For to him we may reasonably impute many little inconveniences that we suffer. "I believe" (said that excellent man, the Marquis de Renty, when the bench on which he sat snapped in sunder without any visible cause) "that Satan had a hand in it, making me to fall untowardly." I know not whether he may not have a hand in that unaccountable horror with which many have been seized in the dead of night, even to such a degree that all their bones have shook. Perhaps he has a hand also in those terrifying dreams that many have even while they are in perfect health.

It may be observed, in all these instances, we usually say, "The Devil," as if there was one only, because these spirits—innumerable as they are—do all act in concert and because we know not whether one or more are concerned in this or that work of darkness.

A Few Plain Inferences

There are a few plain inferences for us in these ideas. And, first, as a general preservative against all the rage, the power, and the subtlety of your great adversary, put on the panoply—"the whole armour of God" (Eph. 6:11)— of universal holiness. See that the "mind be in you, which was also in Christ Jesus" (Phil 2:5), and that you walk as Christ also walked, that you have a "conscience void of offence toward God, and toward men" (Acts 24:16). So shall you be able to withstand all the force and all the stratagems of the Enemy. So shall you be able to "withstand in the evil day," in the day of sore temptation, and "having done all, to stand" (Eph. 6:13), to remain in the posture of victory and triumph.

To his "fiery darts"—his evil suggestions of every kind, blasphemous or unclean, though numberless as the stars of heaven—oppose "the shield of faith" (v. 16). A consciousness of the love of Christ Jesus will effectually quench them all.

> Jesus hath died for *you!*
> What can your faith withstand?
> Believe, hold fast your shield! and who
> Shall pluck you from his hand?

If he injects doubts whether you are a child of God or fears lest you should not endure to the end, take to you for a "helmet, the hope of salvation" (1 Thess. 5:8). Hold fast that glad word, "Blessed be the God and Father of our Lord Jesus Christ, which according to his abundant mercy hath begotten us again unto a lively hope . . . to an inheritance incorruptible, and undefiled, and that fadeth not away" (1 Peter 1:3–4). You will never be overthrown, you will never be staggered by your adversary, if you "hold the beginning of [this] confidence stedfast unto the end" (Heb. 3:14).

Whenever the "roaring lion, [who] walketh about, seeking whom he may devour," assaults you with all his malice and rage and strength, "resist [him] stedfast in the faith" (1 Peter 5:8–9). Then is the time, having cried to the Strong for strength, to "stir up the gift of God, which is in thee" (2 Tim. 1:6)—to summon all your faith and hope and love, to turn the attack in the name of the Lord and in the power of His might—and "he will [soon] flee from you" (James 4:7).

But "there is no temptation," says one, "greater than the being without temptation." When, therefore, this is the case, when Satan seems to be withdrawn, then beware lest he hurt you more as a crooked serpent than he could do as a roaring lion. Then take care you are not lulled into a pleasing slumber, lest he should beguile you as he did Eve, even in innocence, and insensibly draw you from your simplicity toward Christ, from seeking all your happiness in Him.

Lastly, if "Satan himself is transformed into an angel of light" (2 Cor. 11:14), then are you in the greatest danger of all. Then have you need to beware, lest you also fall, where many mightier have been slain; then have you the greatest need to "watch and pray, that ye enter not into temptation." And if you continue to do so, the God whom you love and serve will deliver you. "But the anointing which ye have received of him abideth in you, and ye need not that any man teach you: but as the same anointing teacheth you of all things" (1 John 2:27). Your eye will pierce through snares. You shall know "what is that good, and acceptable, and perfect, will of God" (Rom. 12:2) and shall hold on your way until you "grow up into him in all things, which is the head, even Christ" (Eph. 4:15).

NOTES

NOTES

NOTES

NOTES

Additional Sermon Resources

Great Women of the Bible   **Clarence E. Macartney**
A collection of sermons from a master pulpiteer of yesterday. Macartney's unique descriptive style brings these women of the Bible to life and provides inspirational reading for all Christians.
ISBN 0-8254-3268-5   **208 pp.**   **paperback**

The Greatest Questions of the
Bible and of Life   **Clarence E. Macartney**
Discussing questions such as What shall I do with Jesus? What must I do to be saved? If a man dies, shall he live again? and Barabbas or Jesus? Clarence E. Macartney challenges his readers to ask questions, seek the answers from the pages of Holy Scripture, and employ this method of teaching in his or her own situation to great profit.
ISBN 0-8254-3273-1   **192 pp.**   **paperback**

Greatest Texts of the Bible   **Clarence E. Macartney**
This collection of sermons represents some of the author's strongest and most impassioned preaching. Except for slight modifications and updating, and the insertion of Scripture references where needed, these sermons are reissued in their original form.
ISBN 0-8254-3266-9   **208 pp.**   **paperback**

The Greatest Words in the Bible and in
Human Speech   **Clarence E. Macartney**
A group of fifteen sermons based on fifteen words and their corresponding biblical meaning and significance. Macartney explores such words as: sin, forgiveness, now, whisperer, tomorrow, why, repent, heaven, memory, prayer, death, and experience.
ISBN 0-8254-3271-5   **192 pp.**   **paperback**

He Chose Twelve   **Clarence E. Macartney**
This careful study of the New Testament illuminates the personality and individuality of each of the Twelve Disciples. A carefully crafted series of Bible character sketches including chapters on all the apostles as well as Paul and John the Baptist.
ISBN 0-8254-3270-7   **176 pp.**   **paperback**

Paul the Man   **Clarence E. Macartney**
Macartney delves deeply into Paul's background and heritage, helping twentieth-century Christians understand what made him the pivotal figure of New Testament history. Paul's life as missionary and theologian is carefully traced in this insightful work.
ISBN 0-8254-3269-3   **208 pp.**   **paperback**

Twelve Great Questions
About Christ   **Clarence E. Macartney**
Macartney addresses commonly asked questions about the life and person of Jesus Christ. The integrity and inspiration of the Scriptures underlies the provocative answers that Dr. Macartney provides in this thoughtful book. The broad range of subject matter will inform and inspire laymen and clergy alike.
ISBN 0-8254-3267-7   **160 pp.**   **paperback**

Treasury of the World's Great Sermons **Warren W. Wiersbe**
These outstanding sermons are presented from 122 of the greatest preachers. A short biographical sketch of every preacher is also included. Complete with an index of texts and sermons.
ISBN 0-8254-4002-5   **672 double-column pp.**   **paperback**

Classic Sermons on the Attributes of God   **Warren W. Wiersbe**
These classic sermons lay a solid foundation for the study of God's attributes such as truth, holiness, sovereignty, omnipresence, immutability, and love. Includes messages by Henry Ward Beecher, J. D. Jones, J. H. Jowett, D. L. Moody, and John Wesley.
ISBN 0-8254-4038-6   **160 pp.**   **paperback**

Classic Sermons on the Birth of Christ **Warren W. Wiersbe**
The central theme of the Bible is expanded and expounded in
this collection of sermons from such great preachers as Henry
P. Liddon, Walter A. Maier, G. Campbell Morgan, Arthur T.
Pierson, and James S. Stewart.
ISBN 0-8254-4044-0   **160 pp.**   **paperback**

Classic Sermons on Christian Service   **Warren W. Wiersbe**
Dynamic principles for Christian service will be found in these
classic sermons by highly acclaimed pulpit masters. Warren W.
Wiersbe has carefully selected sermons which describe the
essential characteristics of Christian servanthood.
ISBN 0-8254-4041-6   **160 pp.**   **paperback**

Classic Sermons on the Cross of Christ **Warren W. Wiersbe**
An inspiring collection of sermons on perhaps the most
significant event the world ever experienced—the death of
Christ. Through masterful sermons by great pulpit masters, the
reader will gain a greater understanding of the theological,
devotional, and practical importance of the cross of Christ.
ISBN 0-8254-4040-8   **160 pp.**   **paperback**

Classic Sermons on Faith and Doubt   **Warren W. Wiersbe**
A collection of 12 carefully selected sermons, the goal of which
is to stimulate the growth and maturity of the believer's faith.
Among the preachers represented are A. C. Dixon, J. H. Jowett,
D. Martyn Lloyd-Jones, G. Campbell Morgan, and Martin
Luther.
ISBN 0-8254-4028-9   **160 pp.**   **paperback**

Classic Sermons on Family and Home **Warren W. Wiersbe**
The erosion of traditional family and biblical values is
accelerating at an alarming rate. Dr. Wiersbe has compiled the
best of classic sermons on family life to help recapture God's
enduring truth for the family today.
ISBN 0-8254-4054-8   **160 pp.**   **paperback**

Classic Sermons on Hope   **Warren W. Wiersbe**
Crime. Poverty. Disease. Loneliness. Social upheaval. Warren
W. Wiersbe has chosen twelve classic sermons on hope that
will encourage the reader to face life's struggles with a confident
Christian hope. Included are sermons by G. Campbell Morgan,
D. L. Moody, Charles Spurgeon, and A. W. Tozer. Excellent
starter material for sermon preparation; solid spiritual content
for devotional readers.

ISBN 0-8254-4045-9   **160 pp.**   **paperback**

Classic Sermons on the Names of God   **Warren W. Wiersbe**
Any study of the names of God in Scripture will be enhanced
by the classic sermons included in this collection. They feature
sermons from Charles H. Spurgeon, G. Campbell Morgan, John
Ker, George Morrison, Alexander MacLaren, and George
Whitefield.

ISBN 0-8254-4052-1   **160 pp.**   **paperback**

Classic Sermons on Overcoming Fear   **Warren W. Wiersbe**
Classic sermons by such famous preachers as Alexander
Maclaren, V. Raymond Edman, Clarence Macartney, George
H. Morrison, Charles H. Spurgeon, George W. Truett and others.
Wiersbe has chosen sermons which offer insight as well as
hope for believers faced with the uncertainty of this pilgrim
journey.

ISBN 0-8254-4043-2   **160 pp.**   **paperback**

Classic Sermons on Prayer   **Warren W. Wiersbe**
Fourteen pulpit giants present the need for and the results of a
life permeated with prayer. These sermons by such famous
preachers as Dwight L. Moody, G. Campbell Morgan, Charles
H. Spurgeon, Reuben A. Torrey, Alexander Whyte, and others,
will help you experience the strength and power of God in
prayer.

ISBN 0-8254-4029-7   **160 pp.**   **paperback**

Classic Sermons on the Prodigal Son   **Warren W. Wiersbe**
These sermons by highly acclaimed pulpit masters offer unique
insights into perhaps the most famous of Christ's parables.

These sermons will provide new understanding of the relationships between the son, father and other son. Believers will also be challenged to apply the wonderful truth of the Father's love to their own lives.

ISBN 0-8254-4039-4   **160 pp.**   **paperback**

Classic Sermons on the Resurrection of Christ   **Warren W. Wiersbe**
These sermons represent the best in scholarship, warmed by deep inspiration and enlivened by excitement about what the Resurrection of Christ means to the believer.

ISBN 0-8254-4042-4   **160 pp.**   **paperback**

Classic Sermons on the Second Coming and
Other Prophetic Themes   **Warren W. Wiersbe**
The second coming of Christ is a promise presented in many New Testament passages. Dr. Wiersbe has marshaled an array of classic sermons on Christ's coming by great preachers such as C. H. Spurgeon, G. Campbell Morgan, C. E. Macartney, and Alexander MacLaren.

ISBN 0-8254-4051-3   **160 pp.**   **paperback**

Classic Sermons on the Sovereignty of God   **Warren W. Wiersbe**
Sovereignty. All authority, power, dominion, and majesty belong to God. Warren W. Wiersbe has chosen twelve classic sermons that capture the glory and grace of this divine attribute. Included are sermons by Paul Little, R. A. Torrey, C. H. Spurgeon, and Jonathon Edwards.

0-8254-4055-6   **160 pp.**   **paperback**

Classic Sermons on Spiritual Warfare   **Warren W. Wiersbe**
In a timely new compilation of classic sermons, Dr. Warren Wiersbe offers eleven expositions dealing with various facets of Satanic activity. Included are sermons by such outstanding preachers as William Culbertson, Allan Redpath, D. Martyn Lloyd-Jones, G. Campbell Morgan, and C. H. Spurgeon.

ISBN 0-8254-4049-1   **160 pp.**   **paperback**